Pamela Coleman Smith & Madge Gill

*Astrology
Second-Sight
Art*

ANDREA J. MILES

GREEN MAGIC

Pamela Coleman Smith & Madge Gill © 2023 by Andrea J. Miles.
All rights reserved. No part of this book may be used
or reproduced in any form without written permission
of the Author, except in the case of quotations
in articles and reviews.

GREEN MAGIC
Seed Factory
Aller
Langport
Somerset
TA10 0QN
England

www.greenmagicpublishing.com

Designed and typeset by Carrigboy, Wells, UK.
www.carrigboy.co.uk

ISBN 978-1-915580-10-8

GREEN MAGIC

"The position of the artist is humble.
He is essentially a channel."
Piet Mondrian

DEDICATION

This book is dedicated to Pamela Colman Smith and Madge Gill.

THANKS GO TO

Mark Hetherington, for technical support with images and photography.

Kevin Rowan Drewitt, for proofreading and suggestions, as well as astrological mathematics and overall enthusiasm for the project.

Paul D. Knight, for all the support and laughs along the way during the process of writing this book.

There are many other people to thank who have assisted in various ways with the chapters and each of them is acknowledged in the relevant chapter.

Lastly, I would like to acknowledge the continuous friendship, love and support from the following people whose encouragement and kindness over the last few years has been invaluable:

Joel Clark, Sarah Dowding, Diane Hollingworth,
Andrew Jenkins, Paul Olford and Kathy Rowan.

Contents

PAMELA COLMAN SMITH 1878–1951 — 7
  Biography — 9
  What Pamela Colman Smith's Rectified Natal Chart Shows — 25
  Alienation, Distinction and Friendship — 30
  Children, Performance and Service — 35
  Psychic Sensitivity, Hidden Depths and Relationships — 39
  Creatives, Production and Synaesthesia — 45
  A Spiritual Quest, Fame and Heritage — 50
  Futurism, Humanity and Inspiration — 56
  Belonging, Self-Expression and Suffrage — 59
  Frustration, Quick-Thinking and Publishers — 61
  Realism And Restlessness, Making Changes and Working Hard — 64
  Recognition, Diligence, Environment and the Rider-Waite Tarot Deck — 68
  Responsibility, Sacrifice, Awareness and Fundraising — 75
  Entertainment and Hospitality — 78
  Purpose and Spiritual Fulfilment — 82
  Closing the Circle — 84
  Acknowledgments, Credits and References — 88
  Astrology detail — 89
  Blog — 89
  Books — 90
  Magazines — 91
  Newspapers — 91
  Pdf — 92
  Websites — 92

CONTENTS

MADGE GILL 1882–1961 — 94
- Biography — 94
- Astrology in Action — 117
- What Madge Gill's Rectified Natal Chart Shows — 117
- Capricorn, Saturn and Relationships — 120
- Appearance and Impression — 123
- Skill, Initiative and Success — 125
- Restlessness and Willfullness — 128
- Distiction and Independence — 130
- Culture, Philosophy and Religion — 133
- Being an Outsider Artist — 136
- Feelings and Nurturing — 137
- Communication, Mercury and Variety — 140
- Children and Creativity — 143
- Mind Matters and Psychic Ability — 146
- Working With Spirit Energy — 148
- Belief, Calling, Freedom and Truth — 152
- Saturn Appears as Life Closes for Madge Gill — 155
- Acknowledgments, Credits and References: — 162
- Astrology detail — 165
- Books — 165
- Journals — 165
- Magazines — 166
- Newspapers — 166
- Pdfs — 166
- Reports — 166
- Websites — 166

GLOSSARY OF TERMS — 169

CHAPTER ONE

Pamela Colman Smith 1878–1951

Artist of the Rider-Waite Tarot Deck, Costume & Stage Designer, Folklorist, Illustrator, Psychic, Storyteller, Publisher and Suffragette

From *The Craftsman*, 1912.
www.commons.wikimedia.org public domain.

Pamela Colman Smith is best known for being the artist for the *Rider-Waite Tarot Deck*, which was released in 1909 by London publisher, William Rider, and conceived by author and mystic, Arthur Edward Waite (also known as A.E. Waite). When the tarot cards were published, Smith's name was omitted from the title of the deck. This was likely due to the discriminatory and patriarchal culture of Britain at the time. Smith signed her initials

'PCS' in black at the bottom corner of the cards (excluding The Fool card), thus showing ownership of her artwork. The image of her initials resembles the ancient symbol of a caduceus – the staff carried by Hermes in Greek mythology.

Waite died in 1942 and towards the end of his life he recognised that out of all his ambitious projects, the tarot deck was his most fruitful project (Waite, 1995, x). However, he barely mentioned Smith in his autobiography, *Shadows of Life and Thought*. Smith struggled financially throughout her life and received no copyright or credit for her contribution to the tarot cards. Furthermore, she was only paid a nominal amount for her part in creating the *Rider-Waite Tarot Deck*.

Over 100 years after the original *Rider-Waite Deck* was published, the *Smith-Waite Tarot Deck Centennial Edition* was released by U.S. Games Systems, Inc. It is a faithful reproduction of the original Rider-Waite cards. Rider's name was dropped and rightful credit given to Smith's contribution to the 78-card deck. The centennial edition also includes four samples of her non-tarot work, which includes an illustration from Shakespeare's *Much Ado About Nothing* and an illustration from Edwin Waugh's poem, *Christmas Carol*.

More recently, in 2022, *The Weiser Tarot – Arthur Edward Waite / Pamela Colman Smith* was published by Weiser Books. This deck is dedicated to Stuart Kaplan, the head of U.S. Games Systems, who died in 2021, and also Donald Weiser. The latter was a bookseller and publisher at Weiser Books who died in 2017. The colours in this deck are different to the shades and tones originally used by Smith, utilising pastel shades instead of the vibrant colours which were used in the 1909 deck.

Smith's accomplishments during her lifetime were much greater than just her popular designs for Waite's tarot cards. During her most active years, her paintings were exhibited at a variety of galleries in England and the USA, which included major international art-exhibitions (www.lostmodernists.com). In 1907, she was the first female and non-photographic artist to have her work shown at the prestigious 291 Gallery in Manhattan. This venue was managed by the artistic and pioneering photographer, Alfred Stieglitz. Smith's influences are believed to have included Kate Greenaway, William Blake, Walter Crane and Japanese printmakers, such as Hokusai (Katz & Goodwin, 2020, 33).

She also illustrated over 20 books and pamphlets and wrote two collections of Afro-Jamaican Anansi folktales (ibid). Earlier, in 1902 to 1903, she co-edited *A Broad Sheet* with Jack Yeats – brother of the poet, William Butler Yeats. Shortly afterwards, she edited and created *The Green Sheaf* between 1903 and 1904 but, like *A Broad Sheet*, it was short-lived. She went on to manage and own the Green Sheaf Press, which primarily concentrated on women writers and which lasted until 1905 (ibid). Smith was involved with the women's suffrage movement in England, which included creating artwork for the Suffrage Atelier as well as helping working class women attend suffrage rallies (ibid).

Her other successes included costume and stage designs and making miniature toy theatres. In her later years, she managed her large residence in Cornwall, which had servants and visitors as well as a small chapel on the grounds of her land which was for the local Catholic community. Smith was immensely creative, hard-working and original; she was a natural psychic and visionary and was driven to support causes which highlighted inequalities and injustices in society.

For the purposes of continuity, Corrine Pamela Colman Smith (her given name) will now in the main be referred to as 'Smith'.

BIOGRAPHY

Pamela Colman Smith was born Corrine Pamela Colman Smith on 16th February, 1878, at 27 Belgrave Road, Pimlico, which then was in the county of Middlesex and is now in London (G.R.O. BXCJ054463). An advert was placed in *The Standard* newspaper on 19th February, 1878, announcing the birth of a daughter to US citizens, Mr and Mrs Smith (www.britishnewspaperarchive.org.uk). The family moved to Lower Camden in Chislehurst, Kent (Bromley Historic Collections), for a short while and by 1881 they were living in Didsbury, Manchester (ibid). The 1881 Census shows that by this time Smith was three years old and was cared for by her mother and two servants. Interestingly, on that same Census, her mother's date of birth was recorded and the given date of birth made her 30 years old, when really she was approximately 47 years old (www.findagrave.com/). Only Mr Smith as 'Head of the Household' knew why he gave his wife's incorrect age to the enumerator.

In Didsbury, the residents in the other houses on their street were merchants or people who worked in the cotton clothing industry. The Census records show Charles Smith's occupation as 'Merchant – American Trade', which shows he was living there for business purposes. Presumably, he was successful as the family lived there for several years.

Mr. Smith's daughter died in Bude; Cornwall on 18th September, 1951, aged 73. Her death certificate records her name as 'Corinne Pamela Mary Smith'. The name 'Mary' she may have added by deed poll when she converted to Roman Catholicism in 1911 (Kaplan & Foley O'Connor, 2018, 344).

When she lived in London, she dropped the name Corrine but started using it again when she moved to Cornwall. The cause of her death is recorded as 'myocardial degeneration', which is heart muscle weakness. This is caused by the cardiac muscle becoming enlarged, which makes it rigid (Robinson, 2016, 49, 187). As we already know, Smith's parents were Charles Edward Smith, a merchant, and her mother was Corrine Colman Smith. Their daughter was an only child who was born eight years into their marriage when Mr Smith was 31 and Mrs Smith was 43 years old. The Smiths did have a son who was born in Brooklyn, New York, in 1873 but sadly he died in the same year (possibly at birth, although this is speculation). He was buried in Brooklyn and he was named Charles Smith (www.findagrave.com).

Smith's parents both came from prominent families who lived in Brooklyn Heights, New York. Her maternal grandfather was Samuel Colman and he was a well-known bookseller, publisher and etcher in Boston and New York City (Kaplan & Foley O'Connor, 2018, 15). Smith's maternal grandmother was Pamelia Chandler Colman who was a prolific author of children's books, many of which were collections of translated French and German fairy tales (ibid). The Colman family were members of the Swedenborgian New Church (ibid) which was founded by the Swedish mystic and philosopher, Emanuel Swedenborg. Pamelia's son, Samuel Colman, was an artist, global traveler and zealous collector of Chinese and Japanese prints, a passion which was shared by his niece and is reflected in some of her art (ibid).

Smith's mother was not as renowned as her uncle, Samuel. However, she was described by newspapers as "a great drawing room actress of Brooklyn" who was "very beautiful" (ibid). Clearly, she enjoyed performance and this was mirrored by her daughter. When Smith lived in London, she would open her studio to an invited audience, where she appeared in costume and entertained with her storytelling.

PCS's mother, Corrine Colman Smith. www.findagrave.com – Memorial ID – 205139046.

Her paternal family were prominent for their contribution to business and government. Her paternal grandmother, Lydia Lewis Hooker, was a direct descendant of Thomas Hooker, who was a Puritan clergyman and a co-founder of the Connecticut Colony (Kaplan & Foley O'Connor, 2018, 16). This was originally an English colony in New England, which is in the northeast corner of the United States.

Smith's paternal grandfather, Cyrus Porter Smith, was an integral figure in developing Brooklyn in the early nineteenth century. It went from being a small village to an active and lively borough. His achievements in government included being appointed Mayor of Brooklyn as well as serving as a State Senator of New York. He was also an entrepreneur and his successes included helping to found the first gas company in Brooklyn, he was also director of Brooklyn's Union Ferry Company. An older son, Bryan, followed Cyrus into the line of business and was equally successful (ibid).

Smith's father, Charles Edward, was the youngest son of Cyrus Porter Smith. According to a newspaper report in the *Brooklyn Daily Eagle* in 1904, Charles Edward was an "artist rather than businessman" and "hardly met with the material success of his brother." The same article reported that Charles Edward spent a lot of time in London and that he was employed for a short while by an eminent London design firm, Nichols, Colshaw & Co. (ibid). Bryan and Charles Edward had a brother called Theodore who was close to Charles Edward and his daughter. When Smith's uncle died, he left a significant inheritance to her (ibid).

As previously discussed, by 1881 Mr and Mrs Smith and their daughter were living in Didsbury, Manchester, England, where Smith's father was employed as a manufacturer of upholstery (Kaplan & Foley O'Connor, 2018, 16). Several years later, the family moved to Jamaica where Charles Edward took employment as an auditor with the West India Improvement Company. This was a business that completed the railroad on the island from the colonial government (ibid). Smith would often return to New York during this period of her father's employment and where she was "under the entire charges of a Jamaica negro (sic) nurse" (ibid). Smith visited several homes in Brooklyn Heights while she was in New York, presumably with family and friends of the family.

In 1893, when Smith was fifteen, she enrolled to study art at the Pratt Institute in Brooklyn. Her registration card showed that the purpose of her studies was for art teaching or illustration (Kaplan & Foley O'Connor, 2018, 17). However, in the summer of 1896, when Smith was eighteen years old, she had to return to Jamaica to help nurse her sick mother. Sadly, and shortly after her daughter's return to Brooklyn, Corrine Smith died, aged approximately 62 years old. Her body was not returned to Brooklyn; instead she remained in Jamaica and she was buried in Saint Andrew Parish Church Cemetery in Kingston (www.findagrave.com).

Smith was then left with the responsibility of running the household in Jamaica for her father, which included paying employers on his estate. Eventually, she returned to New York and she left the Pratt Institute in June, 1897, aged nineteen, without a degree. The transcript of her time at the Pratt Institute reveals that her attendance there was sporadic due to sickness (Kaplan, 2018, 359). However, Smith thrived when she was at the educational establishment and she was inspired by one of her professors, Arthur Wesley Dow. It was through him that Smith became familiar with symbolism and the rising theory about synaesthesia (*see glossary*) (Kaplan & Foley O'Connor, 2018, 17).

In the winter of 1898, Smith and her father went back to Jamaica for a short while, returning to New York in the spring of 1899. The next couple of years were especially productive for her as a New York publisher; R.H. Russell published much of her work. This included issuing *Annancy Stories*, which was a collection of West Indian stories that she had written and illustrated. In Jamaican folk tradition, the Anancy (Smith spelt it 'Annancy') spider is a mischievous spider-god with a human head who is always tricking people to get what he wants. Stories of this character are believed to have originated in the Akan culture in Africa and were transmitted to Jamaica in the transatlantic slave trade (www.jis.gov.jm).

Author's photograph of books 'Annancy Stories' and 'Susan and the Mermaid'.

Long after slavery, Anancy stories continued and were passed down orally through many households. The tales were told during the nighttime and were accompanied by singing. After the singing and storytelling, it ended by the following line being said: "Jack Mandora me nuh choose none." This means: 'no blame shall be attributed to the listener, storyteller or writer' (ibid). Smith was a pioneer in that she is believed to be the first person to have written her own Anancy stories in Jamaican patois and had them published. Frequently, she opened the performance of her Anancy storytelling with the line: "In a long before time – before Queen Victoria come to rein over we" (Colman Smith, 2006, 14). In her book, *Annancy Stories*, her illustrations are also highlighted with a quote in Jamaican Creole. For example: "An him come suddenly 'pon a ting 'pon de ground" (from *Annancy and Dry-Kull*) and "Jus' den Annancy get to de tree bottom" (from *Paarat, Tiger An' Annancy)*.

Her talents did not stop there, for Smith also published illustrations for the play *Trelawney of the Wells* by Arthur Wing Pinero, as well as a commemorative brochure featuring the

PCS's drawing of Ellen Terry and Henry Irving from *The Craftsman*, October, 1912, from article 'A Painter Who Sees Fairies'.

famous Lyceum Theatre actors, Sir Henry Irving and Ellen Terry. She also provided illustrations for a collection of Irish folktales for author Seamus MacManus in *Chimney Corners*. She produced a great deal more, which included a Christmas calendar for 1899 called *Shakespeare's Heroines* (Kaplan & Foley O'Connor, 2018, 27). By the time the calendar was published, she and her father had travelled back to England to promote the *Annancy Stories* and Smith was also seeking employment as an illustrator.

Whilst in London, they made the acquaintance of Bram Stoker, author of the gothic novel *Dracula* who, at that time, was the Business Manager of the Lyceum Theatre. It was through him that Smith was commissioned to provide the illustrations for the aforementioned souvenir brochure. This was to be sold during the Lyceum's forthcoming American tour. Stoker also invited her to join the theatre company on tour as a minor cast

Bram Stoker in 1906, novelist & manager of the Lyceum Theatre.
www.commons.wikimedia.org – public domain.

member; she agreed and enthusiastically took part in crowd scenes. She affectionately called Stoker 'Uncle Brammy' and 'Brammy Joker'.

She remained friends for several years with the company's leading actress, Ellen Terry, and her daughter, Edith Craig (known as Edy). The latter was a socialist and suffragette as well as an actor, designer and producer. She was also the founder and director of the feminist Pioneer Players theatre society for nearly fifteen years. Apparently, it was Edith's mother Ellen who gave Smith the affectionate though apt name of 'Pixie' because of her small height. When she was 38 years old, Smith's passport application form shows her height as being five feet four inches (Kaplan, 2018, 396). It has also been claimed that it was W.B. Yeats who gave Smith the nickname 'Pixie' (Waite, 1995, xiii). Regardless of who gave her the nickname, Smith kept the name, for a while signing some of her letters as Pixie Smith, Pixie and also Pixie Pamela. Her other pen names included: Corrine, Gypsy and Pam.

PCS's passport photo – Image from 'Pamela Colman Smith: The Untold Story'. Used with permission of U.S. Games Systems, Inc. Stamford, CT06902. All rights reserved.

Pixie was a fitting name for her as the Cornish Pixies are believed to be a fairy tribe in the West Country which, as we know, was the area where she spent the second half of her life. Pixie was also apt for Smith because she was captivated by elves, fairies, pixies and mermaids. She believed in fairies as she had seen them when she was in Ireland. While she was there, she became creatively involved with poet and playwright, W.B. Yeats, and his plans for a national Irish theatre. This eventually developed into the Dublin Abbey Theatre (Waite, 1995, xii). One of the reasons why Smith loved the Order of the Golden Dawn was that it took the subject of fairies and the elements seriously (Waite, 1995, xiv). When she was in Ireland she also developed an interest in the Celtic traditions after her experience of seeing fairies. At one point, she was learning Gaelic at the Irish Literary Society in London and this was approximately in 1901. "I go to the Irish Literary on Fridays to a Galic (sic) class – don't learn much, but it's so funny!" (Robinson, 2020, 25).

PCS storytelling using props in a theatrical setting – www.commons.wikimedia.org – public domain. From 'The Lamp' publication, 1903.

Sadly, whilst she was on tour with the Lyceum Theatre in 1899, Smith's father died, which made her an orphan at 21 years old. In 1900, Smith returned to England with her 'new family' the Lyceum Theatre Company and she obtained work with them as an illustrator and set designer. In 1907, she exhibited her watercolours which she had painted. These had been inspired by music; they were shown at the Baillie's Gallery in London and other venues. The paintings made headlines in publications such as *The Illustrated London News* and *The Strand*. Art critic, Frank Rutter, observed that Smith's art was not dissimilar to the stage costume designs of Edward Gordon Craig (Ellen Terry's son) and whom Smith was also friends with.

She also gained a favourable reputation as a storyteller specialising in her West Indian folktales and was a popular entertainer at bazaars, concerts and charity events. As previously discussed, she held open studio evenings, dressed exotically and unconventionally as she performed and told entertaining stories. She had a wide network of acquaintances, contacts and friends.

For a number of years she worked closely with Edith Craig and she was given various roles and responsibilities. For example, Smith assisted with stage costumes in 1901 for a short-lived theatre company called 'Edith Craig & Co.' Later she worked as a designer of exquisite costumes and programmes for productions

Arthur Edward Waite, 1921 – www.commons.wikimedia.org – public domain.

which were staged by 'The Pioneer Players'. Then, in 1913, she worked with Ellen Terry and provided illustrations for her book, *The Russian Ballet*. Some examples of Smith's drawings in this publication include those of ballet dancers, Anna Pavlova and Nijinsky. As noted earlier, in 1903, Smith had launched her own magazine called *Green Sheaf* which ran for thirteen editions; contributors included W.B. Yeats and his brother, artist Jack Yeats, as well as composer, Martin Shaw. For a short while she ran a shop in Knightsbridge where she sold the publication as well as her own artwork (Robinson, 2020, 194).

By 1908, Smith had become a member of the Women's Guild of Arts and it was through this organisation and her friendship with Edith Craig that she came into contact with artists who were working for the suffrage cause. Smith worked in collaboration with artists, Ada Ridley and Alice Woodward, as a stenciller on the book, *An Anti-Suffrage Alphabet*, which was stencilled in green and purple – the suffragette colours. Author, Zoë Thomas, commented on the piece "which sardonically depicted the prevalence of sexist attitudes in society" (Thomas, 2020, 184).

The book was published in 1911 and was designed by artist, writer and social reformer, Laurence Housman, and edited by Leonora Tyson, who was the organiser of the Lambeth/Southwark

Women's Social and Political Union. The book was produced to raise funds for the suffragette campaign and was advertised in *Votes for Women* in December, 1911 (www.artsandculture.google.com). Aside from visiting the USA in 1909 and 1912, Pamela was based in London, primarily in South West London.

The 14th November, 1912 edition of *The Common Cause* magazine stated that Smith was selling calendars, Christmas cards and hand coloured prints at an exhibition organised by *The English Woman* magazine. The aforementioned magazine, *The Common Cause*, was a weekly publication that supported the National Union of Women's Suffrage and was first published on 15th April, 1909. By 1912, Smith had become predominantly known as the illustrator of the *Rider-Waite Tarot Deck*. Her designs took her just under six months to complete (Robinson, 2020, 195), which is an astounding feat.

Smith and Waite had both previously been members of the Isis-Urania Lodge of the Hermetic Order of the Golden Dawn. She joined in 1901, having been introduced to the secret society by W.B. Yeats. Here she became friends with the celebrated actress, writer and women's rights activist, Florence Farr. Whilst she was touring in America with a new art of Irish literary theatre, she met up with Smith who was staying in New York and Smith became her collaborator and stage manager whilst they were both in America.

Eventually, A.E. Waite left the Lodge and formed his own breakaway group which was more focused on mysticism than ceremonial magic. In 1903, Smith joined his order and remained a member until 1909. It was whilst she was a member of Waite's group that she was tasked with the responsibility of illustrating Waite's conceived tarot deck. However, she left the order in 1911, when she converted to Roman Catholicism, because the two were incompatible.

Between 1912 and 1914, she was a regular visitor to Ellen Terry's home in Smallhythe, Kent. During the First World War, Smith started working for the Red Cross charity. She offered

PCS's home – Parc Garland.
Photograph with kind permission from Barry Hodges.

poster designs to them and made toys for Children's Aid (Robinson, 2020, 195). After the outbreak of the First World War in 1914, she took up toy-making. Ever progressive, she held a meeting for the Women's Guild of Art at her studio in 1915, to discuss the possible developments of toy-making. Throughout 1915–1918, Pamela produced posters related to the war effort and relief funds (ibid).

In 1918, having received a significant inheritance from her Uncle Theodore, she moved from London to Cornwall, having bought her first ever home – Parc Garland at The Lizard Peninsula. Surely, this must have been a welcomed form of security for her after years of renting homes in London. This area of Cornwall is the most southerly point of mainland Britain and is bordered with a dramatic coastline, intimate coves and sandy beaches and is a remote area. For approximately eighteen years, Smith maintained Parc Garland, having found her spiritual home there. It was indeed the only home she remained in for a lengthy period of time. This shows how settled she felt there even though it eventually came with financial challenges.

Postcard image of PCS's Catholic Chapel –
with kind permission from Barry Hodges and Hayley White.

The 1921 Census shows that Smith had servants, which included Albert and Nora Lake who were a valet and cook respectively. A 51-year-old Catholic priest a John Aloysius Gibbons was also listed on the Census as well as some other visitors. Interestingly, the 1911 census shows that Mr and Mrs Lake were servants at Nordrach House a sanatorium in Somerset which was built as a Consumption (TB) hospital and which housed 65 people. Previously, Nora had been in service at Somerset for Alfred Elton, a clerk in the holy order she was 19 years old at the time. Eventually, Nora became a lifelong companion to Smith.

There was a small chapel at The Lizard called 'Our Lady of the Lizard' and its' original owner kept it as an open chapel and employed a French abbot there; apparently the chapel was a rented converted building (Robinson, 2020, 156). The owner, Madame Victorine Roberts had business in France and had to return there, no longer able to care for the chapel in The Lizard. Knowing that Smith had bought Parc Garland, she wrote to the Bishop of Plymouth in August 1919 and suggested that if she was

Photo of PCS's fireplace from Parc Garland, now at home in the esoteric bookshop Treadwell's in London. Photo by kind permission of Treadwell's.

willing to take care of the chapel, perhaps it could be transferred onto Smith's freehold property (ibid). Roberts' proposal was obviously conducive to the Bishop as he agreed to her suggestion.

Eventually in 1919 Catholic services began in a building in the grounds of Parc Garland. By the following year Smith was confident with a flourishing congregation of thirty-one people from the local community (ibid). In 1922 Smith wrote to the Bishop expressing her anxiety about her financial challenges which included being unable to pay for Buckfast. This was a tonic wine made by monks at Buckfast Abbey in Devon for the visiting priests (Robinson, 2020, 196) who came to take the services at the chapel.

Unfortunately, Smith experienced financial crisis in 1927 as she had not been able to sell any of her art (ibid). Later in 1939 Corrine (Smith) as she was then calling herself was living with Nora Lake and a couple of other people in Exeter. They were living in "a large mid-terraced residence in a pleasant location at 24 New North Road" (Robinson, 2020, 174). Sadly, the chapel at Parc Garland closed in 1943. It had previously been signed over to the diocese in 1930 (Robinson, 2020, 196). The closure of the chapel was in part due to the larger populated village at nearby Mullion Village which by then had a Catholic church, St. Michael the Archangel (Robinson, 2020, 174), and a constant congregation with regular priests.

Smith and Nora moved from Exeter to Upton, Bude in 1942 and then both moved to a second home in Bude, which was flat number 3 at 2, Bencoolen House (Robinson, 2020, 196). Nora Lake outlived Smith; she died in 1962, aged 88, in a nursing home in Exeter. Alfred Lake, her husband and ex-employee of Smith's, died earlier, in 1937 (GRO at www.ancestry.co.uk).

Mrs Lake had a son called Freddie whom she previously lived with. This was in a bungalow in Bude and the premises were near to the Bencoolen flats where Lake had previously lived with Smith (Robinson, 2020, 137). There is little information available about Freddie other than what members of the local community remember about him (ibid). Perhaps he lived with other family members or, if he was married, lived with his wife at the time when his mother lived with Smith.

On 18th September, 1951, Pamela Colman Smith died aged 73. She had lived with heart problems since 1939 (Robinson, 2020, 196), possibly even earlier for all we know. As noted earlier, her death certificate shows that she died of *'myocardial degeneration'* or heart muscle weakness (Robinson, 2016, 52). Records show that she was buried in the parish of Budehaven on 25th September, 1951, and that her service was taken by a Roman Catholic priest (Robinson, 2016, 49). She was living in poverty at the time of her death so there was no headstone placed on her grave at the Baldhu parish churchyard. The actual plot number would have been recorded in the church records. However, there was a fire there in 1985 and those records were lost forever, leaving it now unknown as to the exact spot where she and others were buried.

WHAT PAMELA COLMAN SMITH'S RECTIFIED NATAL CHART SHOWS

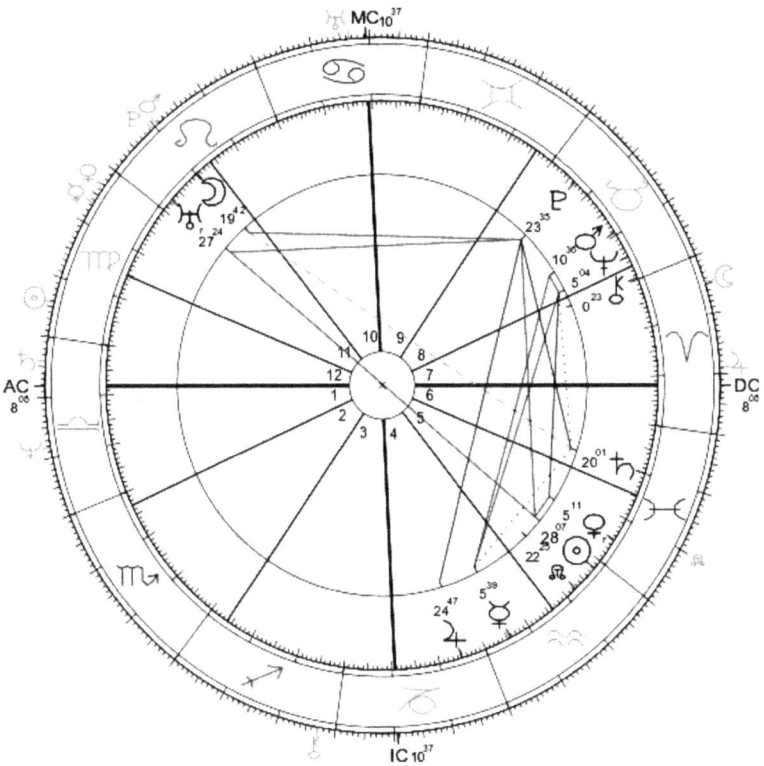

Pamela Colman Smith's rectified natal chart and the transits to it on the day she died on 18th September, 1951.

Corrine Pamela Colman Smith was born on Saturday 16th February, 1878, in Pimlico. Her exact time of birth is unknown. However, using the process of rectification (*see glossary*), a time of birth has been estimated as being 21:00 (9pm). Born under the Sun sign of Aquarius and the Moon sign of Leo, this gives an indication that Smith was creative, original and independent.

Aquarius and Leo belong to the fixed mode (*see glossary*), which suggests that Smith was determined, loyal and tenacious. There is a configuration in Smith's natal chart which is called a

Fixed T-Square and comprises of the Sun in Aquarius, Uranus in Leo and Pluto in Taurus. The focal point in the T-Square is 23 degrees Taurus; and the release point is 23 degrees in Scorpio (*see glossary*). The energy of a fixed T-Square can be determined and purposeful and not easily defeated by challenging situations. Astrologer and author, Frank C. Clifford, observed that T-Squares indicate difficulties and lessons to be learned, yet at the same time "offer great potential for personal growth" (Clifford, 2012, 80).

Two examples of the focal point of Pluto in 23 degrees of Taurus in the eighth house (the area of other people's resources) and the release point of 23 degrees of Scorpio in the second house (of earnings, possessions and values) are borne out by the following: the resource of A.E. Waite's conception of the cards was not financially well paid and it is possible that Smith's earnings were not discussed in detail before she undertook the project. If it was, she may have had misgivings about undertaking the task.

Her anger and frustration about the project is seen in a letter to her friend, the celebrated photographer and modern art promoter, Alfred Stieglitz, when she wrote: "I've just finished a big job for very little cash … Some people may like them" (Kaplan, 2018, 235). She was correct about the latter for not just *some* but *millions* of people enjoyed them and have been helped on their spiritual path to self- discovery through the use of the beautifully illustrated cards. Today, the *Rider-Waite Tarot Deck* remains the world's bestselling pack of tarot cards (Cockcroft & Croft, 2010, 54).

There are three planets in Taurus in Smith's natal chart. The animal and nature-loving side of Taurus can be seen in Smith's design of the *Rider-Waite Tarot Deck*, through the abundance of images related to the natural world. Quite possibly, Smith was inspired by the environments in the different countries and places that she lived. Throughout the tarot deck there are images of meadows, hills and mountains. Also included are the Sun and Moon, sun rays and moonlight, rain, thunder and rainbows as well as ponds, rivers and seas. Not forgetting cat, dogs, fish, horses, lions, snail and lizard. In addition are images of buds, ivy, shrubs and trees, citrus fruits and pomegranates and, finally, a variety of flowers such as lilies, irises, roses and sunflowers. Clearly she found beauty and inspiration from nature and was energised and invigorated by the gifts of Mother Earth.

It is believed that Smith was inspired by the Renaissance *Sola Busca Tarot Deck*; it was the only earlier deck which had full illustrations on the numbered cards. This deck was on display at the British Museum in 1907 (Kaplan, 2018, 352). It seems that Smith was familiar with this deck as she used a few of the Minor Arcana cards as a foundation for her own court cards (ibid), one example being the Queen of Cups. Given that each card of each suit was given a striking and symbolic story, somehow this made the tarot more accessible to use. It was Waite's desire that the tarot deck should not only be used for divinatory purposes. as it had been previously in history, but also for meditation and self-knowledge.

Initially Waite had some unease about Smith working on his set of cards, which apparently was that she had no real understanding about the Greater Mysteries of life to use in connection with the tarot. Apparently, she had to be guided in some of the artwork, especially the Major Arcana. He claimed that "The one thing she lacked was an interest in the meaning of it. With visionaries this is often so," he continued … "They see gods and fairies so vividly that they are completely absorbed in the beauty of the bright forms they see. It never occurs to them to ask 'what does this mean?" (Waite, 1995, xv).

If Waite's comments about Smith not having any real understanding about the Greater Mysteries which were taught in the Order of the Golden Dawn, it clearly was an advantage for him. This is because he realised that Smith was the right person under his guidance to produce a tarot deck because of her artistic, imaginative and clairvoyant abilities (ibid). Susan Wands, author of *Magician and Fool*, wrote that "Pixie was a free spirit who is remembered because she created and left a pack of cards that have ignited our collective imagination" (Kaplan, 2018, 381), which is aptly surmised.

Returning now to the astrology. A second example of how the focal and release point in her natal chart, manifested in her life can be seen by the following. When she inherited a large legacy (an eighth house association) from her uncle, Smith wa sable to buy a large home on a piece of land (a second house connection) and which she owned for over twenty years'

After she died, her solicitors found that she was in debt and owed money to different parties. Her possessions were sold by her solicitors to help pay for various debts which included an unpaid Inland Revenue tax assessment of £688.10 (Robinson, 2020, 187) as well as unpaid wages of £5 and £15 13s 1d owed to the Bude and Stratton District Council for rates (ibid). After all her debts were paid by the solicitors there was nothing left in her estate. This was very poignant as Smith had bequeathed her estate to her dear friend Nora Lake.

In her lifetime, Smith had to work hard to earn money, especially working as an artist which is usually scantily paid. When she lived in Cornwall at her final property, she lived a frugal lifestyle and had not sold any of her art for a long period of time. Overall, she was not a successful business woman and many of her projects were short-lived. In her earlier years, she had clearly become accustomed to a certain lifestyle. For example, when she was a child she always had servants and a nanny to care for her and when she sailed to different countries when she was an adult, she always sailed first class. In addition, when she lived in London she lived in salubrious and wealthy areas of London.

It doesn't appear that she made concessions to save any money or, like many creatives had to find additional work and fill-in jobs outside of the artistic world. It was not uncommon for women not to marry in Smith's lifetime; this was for both companionship and economical reasons. In addition, it was not unusual for a single woman to live with another woman. This was true of Smith, for example, when she lived with Nora Lake in her perennial years as well as living with Mrs Fryer-Fortescue when she lived in Knightsbridge in the early part of the 1900s. Interestingly, the latter (like Smith) was also a member of The Golden Dawn (Kaplan, 2018, 150).

Smith may have become adamant and too fixed in her ways before she finally decided to sell her Parc Garland property in 1942. Had she sold it earlier, she may have avoided being in as much debt. The unyielding nature of the fixed energy is one of the more challenging sides to the fixed T-Square. The Sun in Aquarius and Uranus in Leo positions of the fixed T-Square will be discussed in further detail later on. All in all, there are seven planets in the fixed signs which are: the Sun and Mercury in Aquarius, Mars, Neptune and Pluto in Taurus, the Moon and Uranus in Leo, which indicates an indomitable and determined spirit.

Neptune and Pluto are both outer planets which take a long time to complete a cycle and effect many generations of people. It could be said therefore that Smith was born into a generation that became absorbed with art, magic, poetry, religion and creative writing. This is because the nature of Taurus is 'fixed' and Neptune alludes to the aforementioned subjects. Interestingly, during the 1875–1888 cycle of Neptune in Taurus the following organisations were founded: The Theosophical Society was formally founded in 1875 in New York, U.S.A. and The Blavatsky Lodge of the Society in London was started in 1887, The Society for Psychical Research was founded in 1882 in England and The Hermetic Order of the Golden Dawn was formed in 1888 with its Isis-Urania temple formed in London.

Pluto in Taurus shows that British society was being transformed and that there was a compulsion to unearth societal taboos, using wealth and status to regenerate areas of society in a practical and enduring way. Certainly, during Queen Victoria's reign, society was transformed in many ways with industrial, scientific and technological advances and Smith belonged to the generation which was going to experience this transformation.

Smith's natal chart shows that some of the planets are at home to where they are in the governance of the natural zodiac (*see glossary*). This is shown by: the Sun in the fifth house, Uranus in the eleventh house and Pluto in the eighth house, all of which will be discussed in more detail further on. Principally, it shows that the energy is exceptionally strong in these houses (*see glossary*). Venus is in Pisces and Neptune is in Taurus, which is termed as being in mutual reception – this is when two planets are in each other's sign of rulership. When Venus is positioned in Pisces it is described as being in exaltation (*see glossary*). This means that when Venus is in this sign it finds it very easy to co-operate; the downside of this position can be that there may be challenges in being realistic as well as letting money slip away. Venus in Pisces will be discussed in more detail further on.

On the axis (*see glossary*) of Smith's natal chart, the cardinal signs (*see glossary under 'modes'*) comprise of: Libra AC, Capricorn IC, Aries DC and Cancer MC. This indicates that Smith was driven and self-motivated, particularly in the areas of the self, home, partnerships and career.

ALIENATION, DISTINCTION AND FRIENDSHIP

The Sun, as we already know, was in Aquarius when Smith was born. This shows that she was original, independent, sociable and progressive. The ruler of Aquarius is Uranus and in Smith's natal chart is positioned in the eleventh house. This position suggests that she was open-minded, free-spirited and idealistic. Her principles may have extended to her friendships and at times she could be emotionally detached and unpredictable, such are some of the qualities of Uranus. Her friend and collaborator of the *Broad Sheet*, Jack Yeats, described her as "a little bit erratic," whilst his sister Lily, who was an embroiderer, portrayed Smith as "restless" and "highly strung" (Robinson, 2020, 57).

Despite her flaws, as a companion she gave loyalty and honesty as well as freedom and space to her friends which would have been paramount in any of her relationships, she was free-spirited and independent. Smith has also been described as eccentric, sensitive and changeable (Robinson, 2016, 47) which potentially may have alienated her from people.

Working in groups, communities and societies, she could have mixed in well and thrived with like-minded people and kindred spirits. Although she had this ability for socialising, it could also be said that she was on the margins with different groups and never directly in the limelight with them. However, when she was directly in the spotlight she rose to the occasion, one example being when she was storytelling. Then she became 'a natural' – shining in performance whilst delighting her varied audiences. These included her bohemian friends who were actors, directors, writers and a multitude of other artists and creatives. Being different perhaps afforded her the same recognition as her artistic and creative friends and it is possible that she also craved recognition as a solo performer.

The Sun opposing Uranus aspect is indicative of the afore–mentioned example about Smith's uniqueness but there are other areas where Smith was unable to be categorised and which left some of her contemporaries bewildered. For example, her assumed bi-heritage and sexuality were discussed by those puzzled by her appearance – one example being of Henry Wood Nevinson, who was founder of the Men's League for Women's Suffrage. In his memoir, *Changes and Chances*, he described Smith. She was termed as an "exciting little person" and he "supposed" that she was "touched with negro blood" (Kaplan & Foley O' Connor, 2018, 14). A fellow student of the Pratt Institute and later an advertising executive, Earnest Elmo Calkins, saw Smith perform her folklore stories. In his autobiography, he described her as a "strange African deity." Having earlier read Nevinson's memoirs, he stated that whilst he was unaware that

Smith was of mixed race, it would "account for her peculiar dramatic power" (ibid).

Other comments about her include a newspaper article which reported on how writer, Mark Twain, saw a production of Smith telling her folk stories in America and that "during her narration of them he laughed throughout." The article went on: "… in the weird dialect of the Jamaican negress – a sort of Cockney English with Spanish colouring" (*The Weekly Journal*, 1907, 15). There were other comments too which were more than ignorant. For example, she was also described in the American women's magazine, *Delineator*, as "a brown squirrel, and a Chinese baby, and a radiant morning" (Kaplan & Foley O' Connor, 2018, 14).

Even some of those that became her 'friends' had something to say about her physical appearance. Whether they said it directly to her face we don't know, but certainly in writing there were examples. When W.B. Yeats' father met Smith and her father for the first time he wrote: "Pamela Smith and her father are the funniest looking people, the most primitive Americans possible – but I like them" (Kaplan & Foley O' Connor, 2018, 12). All of these sexist and racist remarks about her show the terminology which is unaccepted today, but was commonly used in Edwardian and Victorian times and this included the stereotypes attributed to people of colour during that period in time.

The speculation about her sexual preferences may have been partly borne out from her remaining unmarried and childless. She had a very close relationship with Ellen Terry's daughter, Edith Craig, who was in long term relationships with Chris St. John (born Christabel Marshall) and Tony (Clare) Attwood – almost a kind of ménage a trois arrangement. Smith stayed for lengthy periods of time at Smallhythe in Kent with this female community.

Craig and St. John were absorbed with dramatic performances which supported the suffrage movement. The two women formed The Pioneer Players in 1911 and between 1915 and 1918

Ellen Terry and PCS outside Anne Hathaway's Cottage in Stratford-upon-Avon. Photo taken by Edith (Edy) Craig. Behind Terry and PCS (*left to right*) are Lindsay Jardine (Edith's close friend) and writer and women's activist, Christabel Marshall, who acted as Ellen Terry's secretary. Under license from the Royal Shakespeare Company/RSC Enterprise Limited.

Smith was a member of the organisation's executive council. Her creative input for the company included costume design for various productions and in 1915 she designed the programme cover for a production called *The Theatre of the Soul*, which was directed and produced by Craig (Kaplan, 2018, 78). Author and scholar, Katherine Cockin, observed that the partaking of "visual artists in The Pioneer Players' productions was significant for the multi-media potential nature of art theatre and its emphasis on the visual" (Cockin, 2001, 177). She described Smith as "the symbolist artist" and also as being an "important member" (ibid) of the group and how she had worked with Edith Craig for a long period of time.

Smith owned her uniqueness and was undeterred by others who found it difficult to categorise and label her. She was a woman who was distinctive and had original talents, virtuous with a good heart. This is an example of how the Sun opposing Uranus in her chart manifested itself in her life and how she never detracted from her determined and optimistic approach to life. It also shows how Smith was open in her thinking by accepting the differences and originality of individuals without any judgment. It has been suggested that the childlike presentation of Smith "was deliberately cultivated as it appealed to those seeking an artist who was tapping into the depths of the psyche" (Katz & Goodwin, 2020, 33). A visitor to Smallhythe, who met Smith there, said of her: "There was something of wildness in her nature, something almost fey" (Katz & Goodwin, 2020, 100). This description of her shows the Uranus energy of being distinctive and true to herself as well as not being chained to any conventions of the time regarding how a woman must behave in British society.

In 1907, the *Brooklyn Life* newspaper reviewed one of Smith's performances of telling Jamaican folk stories. She was referred to as "an artist of quite exceptional brilliancy and absolute originality" (Kaplan, 2018, 249). This quote describes her innovative and novel qualities, which are associated with Aquarians. The following week, the same journal wrote again on Smith's presentation: "Miss Smith's instant success here is a bit unusual. I think it is largely due to her absence of all pose: queer, unexpected, absolutely original as Miss Smith is, one realizes her quite unmistakable genuineness as well as appreciates her talents. She is a gentlewoman, presenting an odd type of thoroughly unconventional femininity – therein lies her greatest charm" (ibid). From these newspaper reports we can see that her distinctive and original style created a buzz in Brooklyn and the audiences valued her alternative and quirky storytelling performances. The Brooklynites must have been very proud of their Miss Smith.

Astrologer and author, Sue Tompkins, observed that people with a Sun / Venus contact in their natal chart (as Smith has) want to be recognised as somebody that is amicable and kind-hearted, anxious to please and wants to be popular especially with women (Tompkins, 1990, 99). Certainly Smith had many female friends and this included being close to celebrated actress, Ellen Terry, and her family, especially Edith (as previously noted).

It is believed by some that Terry acted like a surrogate mother to Smith. However, it is strange that when Terry died in 1928, Smith did not attend her funeral. Perhaps this was due to financial difficulties as well as time limitations and responsibilities at Parc Garland. It could also be that by this time the two women had simply drifted apart. Smith may have previously been merely one of Terry's great theatrical entourage and was a recipient of Terry's 'theatrical luvviness', as were so many others. There appears to be no letters from Terry to Smith, at least not in the public domain. This leaves a void as far as any affection or loyalty is concerned, which is in contrast to the close friendship that Smith had with Terry's daughter, Edith, and her partner. However, through Ellen Terry's letters to her son it is evident that she was indeed impressed by Smith's application and work ethic.

CHILDREN, PERFORMANCE AND SERVICE

The Moon in Leo can indicate some of the qualities of one's mother or the main caregiver. Given that Leo is associated with creativity, entertainment and performance it is interesting that Smith's mother and Terry were entertainers. Researcher and writer, Phil Nortfleet, wrote that: "Corrine Smith is said to have been an avid fan of the London theatre and occasionally performed as a stage diseuse" (Kaplan, 2018, 369). A 'stage diseuse' is an actress who presents dramatic recitals, usually sung accompanied by music; the male counterpart is a diseur (https://www.collinsdictionary.com). Samuel Colman described his sister Corinne as being "an extraordinary singer" (Kaplan, 2018, 356). From these examples we can see the Moon in Leo attributes and qualities borne out by

Smith's mother and supposed 'surrogate mother' being actresses and performers.

The position of the Moon in Leo also indicates that she enjoyed being in the spotlight and playing to an audience. She would have responded well to attention and warmed to admiration and reverence. The Moon in Leo also indicates that she understood the importance of playing and nurturing one's inner child. Although Smith never had children of her own, she liked creating for children and understood the importance of nurturing their imagination. She lavishly illustrated and wrote children's books which must have heartened her own 'inner child'. One example of this being *Susan and the Mermaid*. This book manifests her Venus in Pisces imagination and fantasy beautifully. The story describes Susan's voyage into a magical underworld which was unlocked by her grandmother's magical pearl. There the young girl found a place inhabited by haughty dolphins, genial seahorses and mermaids.

A natal chart does not indicate one's sexual preference(s). However, there is symbolism in Smith's natal chart that suggests she may have been sexually confused and/or ambiguous. This is seen by Neptune positioned in the eighth house. The former is associated with elusiveness and uncertainty, whilst the eighth house is associated with intimacy and sex. Smith may have feared any form of intimacy with either gender, fearing being exposed and vulnerable. If this was true, it would have made it difficult to have some of her emotional needs met.

Neptune in the eighth house can also indicate that one makes sacrifices in the most intimate areas of their life. As far as Smith is concerned, author, Dawn G. Robinson, suggests that Smith may have converted to Catholicism in order "to escape or confine her sexuality" (Robinson, 2020, 128). The idea of sacrifice is also shown by Venus in Pisces in the fifth house, the area associated with love affairs and romance. Neptune is the ruling planet of Pisces and Venus is associated with relationships, as well as money.

It could be argued that Smith's most significant relationship was with the Church, since she was a member of the Catholic Church for over 33 years of her life. Her errand boy in Bude (in approximately 1943) recalled how Smith "was strongly Catholic" and that in Smith's flat "Our Lady would be looking at you" (Robinson, 2016, 48). Smith painted a crucifix on the front of her home but she had to remove it due to complaints, as residents in Bude were mainly Protestant (ibid). Again, Smith in doing this may have found herself detached and on the margins of this small community and certainly the subject of gossip in such a small neighbourhood.

Quite possibly she was considered as shocking and unconventional by painting a crucifix on her front door. These qualities are in keeping with the alternative disposition of Aquarius and Smith would have been adamant to express herself as freely as she wanted to. Her unusual nature is also seen by her trying to encourage her friends in joining the Catholic Church. When she first converted to the religion, which embraces devotions and rituals, she described it as "such good fun" (ibid).

Before she became established in Bude, Smith provided illustrations for the *Way of the Cross* publication in 1917. This was for the French dramatist and poet, Paul Claudel, who was a devout Roman Catholic. Several of his plays were translated and staged by The Pioneer Players society of which Smith was a member. The productions included *The Hostage* (Cockin, 1998, 123) and *The Tidings Brought to Mary*. His verses of a spiritual pilgrimage for *The Way of the Cross* were based on the writings of missionaries, theologians and mystics. Smith was able to blend her passion for creating art along with Catholicism by producing these illustrations for Claudel.

Many commentators have spoken about her unexplained move to Cornwall and undertaking the responsibility of the former mission. However, before she moved to The Lizard and undertook the running of the Catholic church there, she had for several years already been devout and religious. Letters held at the Plymouth Diocesan Archives reveal that Smith was a member of a prayer group called the Confraternity of the Blessed Sacrament. The group raised funds for the improvement of sacramental vessels, and letters reveal that she also identified as "a Child of Mary" and had lived for seven years near Westminster Cathedral (Robinson, 2020, 161). This shows how she feels close to 'Mary' as a spiritual mother, as do most Catholics. However, it may have been of greater meaning and comfort to Smith given that her biological mother had been dead for approximately 25 years by that time.

A letter dated 5th September, 1919, from Monseigneur Henry O'Brien of the Church of the Holy Apostles in Pimlico written to the diocese for The Lizard declared how he valued Smith. He stated that Smith was "an old friend and penitent of mine" and that "what she undertakes to do will be done. I am very sorry to be losing her because she has been a staunch and faithful friend for many years" (ibid). This shows how reliable and trustworthy she was as well as being a committed church devotee who also practiced repentance.

All of this is symbolically illustrated by Saturn in the sixth house and Venus in Pisces in her natal chart. Saturn is associated with being honourable and upright, whilst the sixth house is associated with rituals and service. Saturn is also associated with fear and guilt, which is appropriate to Smith when she attended confession. Saturn and Venus in Pisces provide insight as to how much she took her religion seriously and valued spirituality.

She was a faithful servant to Catholicism until her death; she regularly consulted her Bible, wrote down important passages and frequently doodled images of angels as well as the crucified and risen image of Christ (Kaplan, 2018, 90). In 1939, her biographical details appeared in the 32nd annual volume of *The Catholic Who's Who* (Kaplan, 2018, 344). Irrespective of Smith's devotion to her faith, we can see her Aquarian open-mindedness and ability to accept people who held different religious views to herself. One example of this is connected to her friend Nora Lake, whom she lived with for many years. Lake was a spiritualist and is believed to have attended their meetings at the old Women's Institute in Bude (Robinson, 2020, 137).

PSYCHIC SENSITIVITY, HIDDEN DEPTHS AND RELATIONSHIPS

Smith earlier in her life claimed that she was never a practicing spiritualist but it did seem that she was a channel for spirit through her artwork. She claimed that the strong women and goddesses in her paintings "just came to her" (Kaplan, 2018, 358). Smith was no stranger to psychic activity either. When she lived at Smith Square in London, she lived in a room that had previously been used by a spiritualist. The house was haunted and spirit fragrance of stale incense was experienced and Smith apparently "was said to see and hear all kinds of things" (Robinson, 2020, 105), as did others who also stayed there. Her "friends and acquaintances believed she had a special talent for perceiving directly the spirit world that lay beyond the physical senses" (Greer, 1995, 408). Smith was also aware of her gift for being able to see music as images, for in 1908, she wrote: "Sound and form are more closely connected than we know" (Katz & Goodwin, 2020, 40).

The Venus sextile Neptune aspect in her natal chart also provides insights as to how Smith may have valued her relationships. These include dreaming of love but also having issues about commitments in a relationship. Smith may have sought mystical experiences in her personal relationships; perhaps deliberately she chose celibacy or platonic relationships. As far as anybody knows, there doesn't appear to have been intimate and personal relationships with anyone in her life. Her private life remained so and letters in the public domain never refer to anybody special in her life. Content is usually about work-related matters and there appears to be no books or other literature which refer to anybody speaking about having an intimate relationship with her.

The asteroid Chiron is also known as the 'Wounded Healer' and in a natal chart it represents the area where our deepest wound is and our potential efforts to heal the wound. In Smith's natal chart, Chiron is positioned in the seventh house, the area which governs significant relationships, and it is positioned in Taurus. This is pertinent to Smith in that both the seventh house and Taurus are ruled by Venus in the natural zodiac and are associated with relationships and security. Venus is the ruling planet in Smith's natal chart, by way of Libra being the ascendant – the sign associated with relationships.

Chiron in the seventh house suggests that Smith could have learnt much about herself through significant relationships (both business and personal). She had great charm and popularity and if she was able to recognise that through intimate relationships she could develop and learn much. Through her artistic and creative relationships she may have recognised that she had grown as a person, through the experience and opportunity of having worked closely with another. Through partnerships she achieved effective results whilst still retaining her independence and putting her original stamp on her work. One example being her collaboration with Ellen Terry, when (and as previously noted) she provided the illustrations for Terry's book, *The Russian Ballet*, and where both she and Terry were paid equally.

Astrologer and author, Melanie Reinhart, observed that for people with Chiron in Taurus, some may never "feel solid and safe ... The body may also be feared and controlled rigorously" (Reinhart, 1989, 107). If this was true for Smith, it may add weight to the earlier interpretation of Neptune in the eighth house. There is a conjunction aspect between Neptune and Chiron and Reinhart observed that people with this aspect often respond to interpersonal conflict by "tearful collapse and feelings of being unable to cope" (Reinhart, 1989, 242). She continued that those with Chiron/Neptune aspects often employ "the

Pamela Smith in Private Life.

From 'Private Life' in 1904. www.commons.wikimedia.org – public domain.

hysterical defence of playing victim and 'poor me' if they sense imminent confrontation" (ibid).

A small illustration of this can be seen in the following account by Lily Yeats. She wrote in a letter that she went to see Smith with the intention of colouring her brother Jack's picture for the recent edition of the *Broad Sheet*. Whilst she was doing that, Smith would colour her own picture for the publication. Yeats found Smith to be "clever and charming but lazy" (Robinson, 2020, 57). She claimed that Smith "often lay on the sofa and cried because, she said, I was bullying her and making her work when she did not feel like work" (ibid). This example also shows some of the Moon in Leo astrology in action with 'dramatic emotions', as well as the Chiron and Neptune aspect that Reinhart described.

However, if Lily Yeats regularly turned up unscheduled at Smith's studio with the presumption that colouring the *Broad*

Sheet would take place, perhaps it is unsurprising that her friend did not want to work, particularly if it was an inconvenient time for her and Yeats' visit was unplanned. If it was a regular occurrence that Smith habitually lay on the sofa and cried, then perhaps it was a case of Smith 'playing make-believe with crocodile tears' and seeking attention. This gives credibility to the aforementioned interpretation of the Chiron/Neptune aspect.

The contact between Chiron and Neptune is also indicative of having access to the divine and spiritual realms; this can be through art, meditation, writing and prayer. We know that Smith wrote poetry, one example being the verse called *'Alone'*. This appeared in the fourth edition of the *Green Sheaf* in 1903, when Smith was 25 years old. It is exceptionally poignant (Kaplan, 2018, 52). For example, the last verse of the poem reads: "In cities large – in country lane, Around the world – 'tis all the same; Across the sea from shore to shore, Alone – alone, for evermore" (ibid). The poem is accompanied by a picture (illustrated by Smith) that depicts a woman. She is alone, walking in a barren field with just two trees in it. The narration in the poem expresses grief that, irrespective of where the orator is, they always feel estranged and lonesome.

As previously noted, Smith's friends thought that she was gifted in being able to tune-in to spiritual realms. Often she was oblivious to what she was drawing until afterwards. This gives further credence to the Neptune/Chiron aspect interpretation of Smith having access to spiritual dimensions.

Being a student within The Order of the Golden Dawn involved personal development, which included training practices such as meditation and visualisation. Smith joined the magical society in 1901, when the organisation was just thirteen years old. It was an English secret organisation and permitted women to become members, which was unusual at the time. However, the women in the group were not permitted to the same level of access to all of the teachings that the men did (Willett, 2022, 109–110). Here

Image of part of the church where PCS was converted to Catholicism.
Farm Street Church of the Immaculate Conception in Mayfair.
www.creativecommons.org/licenses – CC by -SA4.0.

was yet another example of the inequality that Smith experienced in her lifetime.

Essential components of The Golden Dawn's teachings included astrology and the tarot. Smith remained at the 'Zelator' level in the group ($1°=10°$). These numbers are significant, for the first digit represents the grade and the second digit the corresponding position on the Hebrew Tree of Life. Zelator is Latin for 'zealot' and derives from the Greek word for 'zeal'. It symbolises the emblematic step into the Golden Dawn teachings and is the preliminary sephirah on the Tree of Life (the Malkuth) which is governed by the earth element. This represents a safe and secure solid grounding for further learning and spiritual advancement (www.mystic.fandom.com). Smith's motto in the group was "Quod Tibi Id Allis" which means: "To yourself as to Other" (Kaplan, 2018, 43).

When she converted to Roman Catholicism, prayer was also part of Smith's daily life, as was attending weekly confession on Saturdays. Relationships with her past friends from the Golden Dawn seemingly evaporated. For example, in 1913, W.B. Yeats' sister Lily wrote of Smith that "she is now an ardent and pious Roman Catholic, which has added to her happiness but taken from her friends. She now has the dullest of friends, selected entirely because they are R.C." (Robinson, 2015, 47). Yeats continued with contempt that her (Smith's) new friends were mainly converts and half educated people (ibid). This suggests that Yeats was missing the old 'Pixie' that she once knew.

There are signals in Smith's natal chart that indicate she was naturally mediumistic and psychic. Interestingly, in a fictional book about Smith called *Magician and Fool* by Susan Wands, the author infers that Smith could see spirit and that her mother knew about her gift. The author developed the fiction further when 'Mrs Smith' said it was an inherited gift in the family (Wands, 2017, 25). Wands may well have touched on a truth in that particular imagining.

Some of the clairvoyant and psychic pointers in Smith's birth chart can be seen by the following astrological data: the Sun and Mercury in Aquarius, as well as Neptune and Pluto in the eighth house. Aquarians are considered to be ahead of their time and this can include seeing into the future as well as experiencing and seeing phenomena or unusual things that others cannot. Neptune in the eighth house indicates apparitions that may come to fruition. It also suggests clairvoyant dreams and visions, mediumistic abilities and a leaning towards mystery and magic in which representation and symbolism play their part. Smith's dreams were certainly fluent and vivid in her life. In 1904, she wrote to her friend Albert Bigelow Paine that "Lately, I've not seen many visions, but some dreams many and wonderful ... I saw a book in a dream the other day with pictures of 'angels at the well getting water' – very nice!" (Robinson, 2020, 26). This reveals her clairvoyant abilities as well as the rich inner life filled with images and symbolism that she clearly took note of. Pluto is in the eighth house and this position also shows that Smith had strong intuitive feelings and hunches as well as an intense and passionate drive.

CREATIVES, PRODUCTION AND SYNAESTHESIA

With Pluto in Taurus, it could be argued that her passion was channeled into making art that was of practical use. This is because Taurus is an earth sign and in astrology this element is associated with functionality and productivity. Membership of the Arts and Crafts Movement provided Smith with opportunities to rent stalls at the charity bazaars, to sell her arts and crafts whilst raising monies at the same time for charity. She was also able to converse with potential customers and other art workers, making connections and sharing information. Through her membership of the Arts and Crafts Movement, she became friends with artisan, embroidery designer and socialist, May Morris. She was the daughter of the pre-Raphaelite artist and designer, William Morris, and his wife the artist's model, Jane Morris (née Burden).

Smith's practical nature can also be seen with her experience and knowledge of theatre in an article which appeared in a supplement to the *New Age* publication in 1910. There she talks about the practicalities in a theatre community, knowledge of a working theatre and the importance of behind-the-scenes creatives such as costumiers, designers and wardrobe mistresses; as well as the importance of effective communication within the team. She also discusses practical topics such as care and repair of costumes, different materials and how the players wear costumes.

She also stated: "What a useful thing a dramatic library would be. In such a place, students of the drama, actors and producers, designers and others could easily refer to valuable material" (Kaplan, 2018, 289). One senses some frustration from her as she continued in the article: "At present, it takes endless trouble and time to find what is wanted in a library or museum." She illustrates her point by the following example: "Where would one look for the dress of a Jewish woman in England in the year

PCS looking over her shoulder. Photograph by Gertrude Kasebier.
www.creativecommons.org – public domain.

1185?" (ibid). This shows not only the practical side of her nature but also how she valued the behind-the-scenes creatives in the theatre (symbolised by Venus in Pisces in her natal chart), as well as the importance of authenticity and detail to help create an illusion as indicated by Saturn in Pisces in the sixth house.

Returning to the position of Pluto in Taurus, it also indicates that Smith could be drawn towards the occult or as A.E. Waite termed it: 'The Secret Tradition'. Pluto in the eighth house is also associated with transformation so, in terms of any mediumistic abilities she may have had, it suggests that she could 'transform' through trance. One example being trance mediumship – whether she did ever did undertake the experience of trance mediumship we do not know but it seems unlikely, at least not in terms of demonstrations for sitters. As we already know, she did say that she was not a practicing spiritualist, although she may have been in a semi-trance when creating some of her art.

Pluto and the eighth house are both associated with physical and metaphorical death, whilst Neptune is associated with spirit and the ether. It could be argued that Smith produced psychic and spiritual art. Mercury square Neptune in her natal chart signals that she could correspond with inspiring words (both spoken and written), conveyed images through words as well as communicate through the form of art. Overall, she was highly creative in non-verbal communication. The Mercury square Neptune aspect also suggests that her mind needed to be inspired and that she needed a vehicle for her imagination.

Certainly, art, design, music, painting and writing provided her with an outlet for her creativity and sensitivity to music. In January, 1907, the *Brooklyn Life* newspaper reported that "She commenced to draw pictures as soon as she could hold a pencil" (Kaplan, 2018, 248), showing what a keen and natural artist she was as a child. The newspaper went on to say that "After an evening at the opera or concert, she will sometimes work all night, not illustrating the music she has heard, so much as the thoughts suggested, and these paintings she calls musical symphonies" (ibid).

This was an important key to Smith's artistic faculty, her ability to visualise music is a form of synaesthesia. This is a condition whereby two or more of the main five senses (that are usually experienced separately) are automatically and involuntary joined together. For example, some synaesthetes experience colour when they hear sounds or read words in the air. For Smith, it was experiencing colour and shapes when she heard classical music. In 1908, a Welsh newspaper, *The Cambria Daily Leader*, included an excerpt from *The Strand Magazine*. It asked the reader if they possessed "this peculiar psychic gift – this power of conjuring up music with pictures" (*The Cambria Daily Leader*, 1908, page unnumbered).

The UK Synaesthesia Association describes the condition as a union of the senses and explains it is an automatic condition which cannot be turned on and off (https://uksynaesthesia.com). Interestingly, contemporary research has found that people on the autistic spectrum have a greater than average chance of having synaesthesia (https://embrace-autism.com).

ASTROLOGY SECOND SIGHT ART

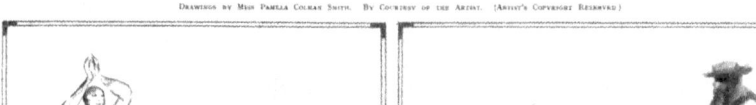

Images of PCS's automatic impressions – from 'The Illustrated London News' February 12th, 1927. © Mary Evans Picture Library.

Photo of Edward Gordon Craig.
www.commons.wikimedia.org – public domain.

In February, 1927, *The Illustrated London News* featured and reported on Smith's "Remarkable 'Visions' of Music: 'Automatic' Impressions". Art critic and art historian, Charles Lewis Hind, described Smith's drawings which appeared in the aforementioned publication as "signposts on a bye-path to the future." Certainly her designs for the tarot cards were futuristic given, as we already know, that the *Rider-Waite* cards are the fastest selling tarot deck (Cockcroft & Croft, 2010, 54).

Apparently, Smith had her first 'music picture' vision in 1900, on Christmas Day, when she was at Ellen Terry's house and was listening to Edward Gordon Craig playing Bach on the piano (Kaplan, 2018, 60). She vividly remembered the experience and in the interview for *The Illustrated London News revealed that* "a shutter clicked back and left a hole in the air about an inch square, and through it I saw a bank and broken ground, the smooth trunks of trees with dark leaves; across from left to right came dancing and frolicking little elfin people with the wind blowing through their hair and billowing their dresses" (ibid).

She continued to explain how clear and vivid the picture was, its beautiful colours and just as she was finishing the drawing, very quickly "the shutter clicked back again" (ibid). However, she did not continue with the 'music pictures' until two years later. This was triggered again when she started to attend concerts given by the composer, Arnold Dolmetsch.

French music critic, Georges Jean-Aubrey, observed Smith producing her 'music pictures' and described the process in the following way: "She comprehends music visually, whether a symphonic piece or a composition. For her, the musical impression is immediately transformed into a graphic image" (ibid). He continued that he had "seen her curled up in a corner at a concert with her sketch book on her knees, a sepia brush in her hand, listening to the work" (ibid).

Composer, Claude Debussy, said of his friend Smith that her drawings to his compositions were his dreams made visible (Kaplan & Foley O'Connor, 2018, 62). Smith told *The Strand* publication in 1908 that "what I see when I hear music – thoughts loosened and set free by the spell of sound" (Kaplan & Foley O'Connor, 2018, 63). She also likened her visions to "unlocking the door into a beautiful country" (Kaplan & Foley O'Connor, 2018, 65), which may have been the spirit world. Many people who are sensitive to spirit realms have spoken about the beautiful vibrant colours they experience, perhaps through dreams, an epiphany and also a near-death experience. They observe that the spirit world is so very different to the material world, certainly in terms of atmosphere, colour and music.

A SPIRITUAL QUEST, FAME AND HERITAGE

Smith was described by critic and journalist, Benjamin De Casseres, as being "a blender of visions, a mythic and a symbolist, one who transfigures the world she lives in by the overwhelming simplicity of her imagination" (Kaplan & Foley O'Connor, 2018, 69). This

'Spring Song' watercolour executed in 1907, painting inspired by Edvard Grieg's classical composition Våren. Under license from Tate Images.

indicates the artistic, mystical and spiritual side of Smith's nature, which is encased in the astrological data of her natal chart of the Moon in Leo, Venus in Pisces and Neptune and Pluto in the eighth house. Her watercolour 'music pictures' were exhibited in Belfast, Cambridge, Edinburgh, London, Paris and Belgium.

Returning again to astrological data, Jupiter and Uranus are both trine Chiron in Smith's natal chart. This aspect suggests that Smith may have been restless and unsettled for a long period in trying to ascertain what her real purpose in life was. Jupiter is associated with exploration and questing, religion and travel (mentally and physically), higher education and politics.

We know that her life was touched by all of the aforementioned subjects. While she was busy living her extensive lifestyle, she may have believed there was a guiding higher force at play which would get her to where she was meant to be in life and reveal what her purpose was. Certainly, she experienced fame as well as success in her younger life, which eventually drained away. For the last 30-plus years of her life, she lived virtually in social isolation.

There is a further contact with Chiron, which is the Sun sextile Chiron. Astrologer and author, Barbara Clow, observed of this aspect that it produces a profound depth at an early age, an environment which offers to develop high principles, and a great need to bring a significant work into the world (Clow, 2007, 131). What defines 'an early age' we do not know, but perhaps Smith's nanny and nurse who cared for her when she was in her formative years were religious and their beliefs and faith may have influenced her. Given that Chiron is positioned in the seventh house and made various contacts with other planets, it could be argued that Chiron could also be associated with Smith's parents' marriage. She may have observed that it wasn't a particularly close and intimate partnership (if it was) and that it brought certain burdens and responsibilities – something which she did not want for herself.

Returning once again to the Sun opposing Uranus aspect, this also indicates a strong urge to break free from any traditions and values that she was born into with a defiance to be different. This we can see through Smith not marrying and, unlike her mother, she did not have to follow a husband around because of his employment. This involved not only moving, but going to different countries and, as we know of Charles and Corrine Smith, they lived in England, Jamaica and New York because of his work. This set-up with a partner may have infringed upon Smith's idea of freedom and independence, unless of course she was able to take a partner who was as independent as she was and/or who understood her need for space.

However, there are indications in Smith's natal chart and examples throughout her life where she did inherit certain family traditions. This is seen by Jupiter being positioned in the fourth house – the area associated with family, heritage and legacy. Mercury is also in the fourth house and its associations include commerce, transportation and communications. Jupiter's associations include, fame, politics, religion and publishing.

As we have already heard, different branches of her family were religious; the faiths included the Swedenborgian New Church, Puritanism and Smith's conversion to Catholicism. Before she converted to the religion, she may have been interested in the Rosicrucian Enlightenment which professed mystical and spiritual wisdom. This was an area that her collaborator, W.E. Yeats, was passionate about. In 1915, he formed *The Fellowship of the Rosy Cross* and later wrote about *The Brotherhood of the Rosy Cross*.

Approximately eight years before she converted to Catholicism, a photograph of Smith appeared in *Chassell's Magazine*. The article was headlined: 'The Woman Editors of London-Miss Pamela Coleman (sic) Smith' and the photograph taken by her publishers, Russell & Bros (Thomas, 2020, 169). She was wearing a demure dress with a lace collar as well as a shawl and two necklaces, each with a cross on them. If the necklaces were not worn for publicity reasons, this suggests an interest of a structured religion before she finally converted to Catholicism. It has been suggested that this particular image "exemplifies a common approach used by art workers: she is removed from the business context, instead portrayed as the height of feminine sophistication" (Thomas, 2020, 168). Clearly, this photograph is in contrast to the ones of Smith dressed in character for performance as storyteller for her *Annancy Stories*.

The Jupiter subjects of celebrity and recognition in the family can be seen by Smith's posthumous fame as the illustrator of the *Rider-Waite Tarot Deck* and also by her father's cousin, William Hooker Gillette. He was a famous actor and playwright and is best known for playing Sherlock Homes on stage in the 1890s. Smith produced five illustrations of Gillette, of which two portray him as Sherlock Holmes (Kaplan, 2018, 138).

Image from 'Pamela Colman Smith: The Untold Story'.
Used with permission of U.S. Games Systems Inc., Stamford, CT06902. All rights reserved.

As we already know, her paternal grandfather was a bookseller and publisher and Smith had her own publishing outlet for her a short while, as well as various business relationships with different publishers. The political association of Jupiter in the fourth house can be seen, not only by Smith's involvement with the suffragette movement, but also by her paternal grandfather's successful involvement in government where he became Mayor of Brooklyn and also State Senator.

In terms of Mercury in the fourth house and its associations with Smith's family, this is borne out by the following: her father was a merchant, her maternal grandmother was an author of children's books and her uncle Samuel (Colman) was a global traveler. Here we can see some of the associations of Jupiter and Mercury inherited by Smith from her family lineage.

William Gillette stage actor 1901 –
www.commons.wikimedia.org-public domain.

The fourth house is also associated with domestic life and the home. Jupiter and Mercury positioned in this region provide some insight into this area of Smith's life. Mercury is also associated with multiplicity and variation, which shows that Smith had many different homes and domestic settings. It also shows that she had a range of different caregivers. This is because the fourth house is traditionally connected with the mother and those who provide care. In contemporary times, families varies in their structure, so it does not always follow that it is the mother symbolised by the fourth house, but in more traditional astrology it was the case.

Smith certainly had a variety of people caring for her when she was a child. For example, when the family lived in Manchester, they had servants and a nanny and when she was an older child and back in Brooklyn, she had a nurse (Kaplan, 2018, 16). Jupiter in the fourth house also suggests that Smith came from a wealthy family. This is because another association of Jupiter is affluence and riches. If they could afford to employ servants and nannies then it shows they were not underprivileged.

Another association of Jupiter is long-distance travel, which was something Smith experienced from a young age travelling to and from England, Brooklyn and Kingston in Jamaica. This may have helped her become more adaptive when it came to her having to travel to different places overseas, as well as moving home many times when she lived in England. It may have added to her feeling like an outsider (if she did), a quality often associated with Aquarians, and where she felt that she didn't fit in with being American, English or Jamaican.

Jupiter is also associated with confidence, optimism and a generosity of spirit as well as the grandiose and expansion. This can be seen by Smith's hospitality towards her friends at her various flats in London, as well as the grand home of Parc Garland in Cornwall. Her home was on two acres of land and she had a small building that she used as her chapel and she also employed some servants who as we know included Mr and Mrs Lake.

Mercury in the fourth house shows that she enjoyed having a home full of people and where people used to come and go. Certainly, that was true when she lived at 84 York Mansions in Battersea Park, London and where she kept a visitors' book. It is famously recorded in her visitors' book on 7th April, 1911, that she revealed she had "had enough of people" and she gave the book to Frederick Allen King, who is believed to be have been her New York agent until the 1930s (Kaplan & Foley O'Connor, 2018, 42). He was also the literary and dramatic editor of *The Literary Digest* (ibid).

FUTURISM, HUMANITY AND INSPIRATION

The position of the Sun in Aquarius indicates that she had lots of friends but was different from the crowd and certainly distinctive. This sign is associated with improving humanity and seeks to make big social changes, sometimes in revolutionary ways. Aquarius is a sign, therefore, that is happy to support any causes that can radically advance humanity. There can be an element

PAMELA COLMAN SMITH 1878–1951

PAMELA COLMAN SMITH
In the costume in which she tells Jamaica folk-tales, collected by herself during a residence on that island

Photo by kind permission of Mary K. Greer at www.marykgreer.com – Source: 'The Literary Digest' July 4th, 1908, photographer Alice Broughton.

of the 'loner' with this sign, irrespective of the sociability of the person. This is because of its futuristic and insightful nature, which potentially can make Aquarians misunderstood as they are more enlightened and insightful than some of their peers, even ahead of their time.

The latter part of this interpretation is echoed in Smith's natal chart by the position of Mercury (the planet associated with communication and mentality) also positioned in Aquarius. This shows that Smith had a bright mind and could pick up new ideas out of thin air which, potentially, made her ahead of her time. Mercury in Aquarius also suggests that she was humorous, quirky and witty; perhaps even slapstick-like at times.

Certainly, Smith seems to have had a degree of telepathic ability, given what Waite said about her when she was creating the tarot deck. In his autobiography, he claimed: "I saw to it, therefore, that Pamela Colman Smith should not be picking up casually any floating images from my own or another mind" (Waite, 2016, 185). This shows not only her faculty of telepathy but also the depth of her psychic abilities. Waite described her as being "a most imaginative and abnormally psychic artist" (Waite, 2016, 184). It has been said that Waite "saw that Pamela, with her clairvoyance, her imagination and her artistic competence, was just the right person to produce, under his guidance, a tarot which would be at once a work of art and a gateway to truth" (Waite, 1995 xv).

The sign of Aquarius is the water-carrier and in the tarot deck this sign is represented by The Star card in the Major Arcana. The symbolism represents giving life and spiritual sustenance to the world; the water from the vessel is washing away the past and making room for a fresh new start where equality and individual freedom can thrive. The glyph for Aquarius is two wavy lines, one on top of the other, and indicates the water and 'making waves'. In other words, the Aquarian can astonish others with something new or different.

The Sun is in the fifth house of Smith's natal chart. This is the area which governs creativity and performance, children and our inner child, as well as romantic liaisons, and the Sun is at home here in the natural zodiac. This position indicates that Smith had a great talent and was determined to get the most out of life and live it to the full. She enjoyed being surrounded by friends and having an adoring audience. This theme is repeated by the Moon being positioned in Leo, for it indicates that Smith loved to be in the spotlight, enjoyed entertaining others and was creative and, where possible, liked to lead and take charge.

She also had the potential to build confidence in others as well as motivate them too. One example of this is borne out when she directed a nativity play for the children of the local primary school when she lived in Cornwall (Kaplan, 2018, 86). Recalling her experience of the production, she said that while the children learned their parts relatively quickly, she called regular rehearsals as she "tried to make it as like the real thing as one could, and the children felt that it was like a 'real live' play, though I think not one of them had ever been in a theatre" (Kaplan & Foley O'Connor, 2018, 87).

This shows what an enthusiastic and instigating mentor she was by introducing the pupils to a new experience whilst teaching them a new discipline. It was an innovative way of her demonstrating to them the importance of team work, something that Smith was more than familiar with. It also shows that she still had creative instincts and brings to mind the information that she inserted on her enrolment card when she enrolled at the Pratt Institute all those years ago, which was that she was considering teaching.

Another idea that Smith conceived and which involved potential students was when she was editor and publisher of the *Green Sheaf* magazine and she opened a school for hand-colouring. The venture was frequently advertised at the back of the publication. It is unknown as to whether Smith ever had any students (Kaplan & Foley O'Connor, 2018, 54) but it was a way of her potentially generating some income. In addition, it would have saved her the task of having to hand-colour each edition herself for the subscribers. Given that the advert was regularly published in the *Green Sheaf*, it does suggest that there was not a big take-up for the opportunity to hand-colour.

BELONGING, SELF-EXPRESSION AND SUFFRAGE

It is possible that Smith also adopted a nurturing role in groups and sought security and a sense of belonging through friends, groups and organisations. This is because the aforementioned areas are indicative of the Moon in the eleventh house respectively. The Cancer/Moon MC (*see glossary*) also suggests that her career may have reflected nurturing qualities such as feeding, housing, nursing and also a sensitivity to the moods of the public and a potential to sway the feelings of the masses.

Certainly, when she was running Parc Garland and the church on her land, we can see the 'caretaking' element. When she was performing and telling stories, she was sensitive to her audience and made the most of areas in presentation such as delivery, timing and silences for an optimum performance. It could be argued that Smith looked to audiences for mothering through seeking attention and approval. Her mother had died by the time she became famous for her wonderful storytelling which both Smith's adult and child audiences warmed to, taking delight in her performances.

The eleventh house also suggests that although she had many acquaintances, she had few genuine and loyal friendships – Nora Lake was one of them, having known Smith for over 30 years and right up until the time that she died. Artists, Alphaeus Philemon Cole and his wife Peggy, were also close friends of Smith. They were regular attendees of Smith's studio parties and their signatures frequently appeared in Smith's visitors' book (Robinson, 2020, 155). It is heartening to see the friendship and love between the three of them. In 1946, irrespective of her failing health, Smith sailed to the US to see the couple. It was the last time she saw them, for she died just a few years later. Perhaps she knew deep down that it would be her final opportunity to see her friends whom she had known for over 40 years.

Like Smith's Moon sign, Uranus is also in Leo and indicates that Smith valued self-expression and lived life creatively and led the way for others through her originality and determination. This is certainly borne out through her illustrations for the *Rider-Waite Tarot Deck*, which is still enjoyed today by both tarot readers and their clients. Her creative input for the suffragette movement, which brought about many changes for women from all classes, is also an example of her assisting others to make progress and improvements to their lives.

In 1911, she was secretary for the Plumstead branch of the Women's Co-operative Guild. She wrote several letters to the Secretary of the National Union of Women's Suffrage Societies, Philippa Strachey. Annoyed and frustrated, Smith was trying to claim back the travel expenses for twelve working-class women who attended a Queen's Hall suffrage meeting (www.lostmodernists.com).

Originally a local suffrage leader had informed them that their bus and train fares would be covered. However, when they arrived at the meeting they were told at the door that their expenses would not be reimbursed and they would have to appeal in writing to Philippa Strachey (ibid). Smith's first two letters were ignored. She was determined, however, and eventually the travel costs were recovered, albeit after some obstruction from Strachey (ibid).

The Plumstead women must have suffered by being financially inconvenienced at that time and probably had to make financial sacrifices elsewhere whilst they awaited their expenses to be reimbursed. Smith was livid about the situation, as well as the incorrect information being given to her from the local suffrage leader to begin with. The motivation by Smith in this example shows how she was willing to fight for the underdog with determination and strength and this can be seen by the symbolism of the Mars conjunct Neptune aspect in her natal chart.

FRUSTRATION, QUICK-THINKING AND PUBLISHERS

The Mercury square Mars aspect in her natal chart reveals that she was capable of venting her frustrations in writing and that she could assert herself through language. This can be seen through letters that she wrote to various people and where she aired her exasperation and irritations. Her letters illustrate anger by her frequently using exclamation marks, incorrect spelling and underlining certain words. This indicates that she may have been impatient and hurried, perhaps even angry, whilst writing some of her letters.

The aspect also suggests that she may have also been less tolerant of people with minds slower than her own, as Mars and Mercury together often indicate quick-thinkers as well as frank-speakers. Some examples of her anger and exasperation can be seen in letters to her close friend, Alfred Bigelow Paine. She vented her anger about being paid small sums by her various publishers and even then she virtually had to force her royalties out of them, after her communications to them were originally ignored (Kaplan, 2018, 44). She referred to one publisher as a "bloomin' (sic) pig" after his poor attitude towards her and her work. She also wrote "Dam (sic) publishers anyway! – I am tired of 'em" (ibid).

With all of these obstacles in her working life, we can also see the presence of Saturn in the sixth house (the area of work) in her natal chart. Some other associations of Saturn include limitation and obstruction, as well as endurance and testing times. In a letter from Ellen Terry to her son, Terry describes how Smith had written to her complaining about her various publishers. She surmised to Terry that it would be easier to have one publisher for all of one's work and to keep on good relations with them the best that one could (Cockin, 2013, 3).

Another interpretation to the Mercury square Mars aspect is that it shows that she was animated, had a competitive mind, was quick thinking and had an ability to easily put thoughts into action. For example, her illustrations for the tarot deck, which compromise of 78 cards, took her just under six months to complete. She was observed several times drawing and painting at an incredibly fast pace. The aspect also suggests that she could easily get bored and had restless energy. If she didn't put her sharp mind to good use then potentially it could result in nagging and being opinionated. It was a wise approach therefore that Smith liked to keep herself busy. Her clear, honest and sharp communication skills can be seen through the way she wrote articles for various magazines and, as we know, she also had an extraordinary imagination when it came to communicating her fictional work and storytelling.

There are other indications in Smith's natal chart, however, which show that she was overall easy-going and not easily angered, which gives a certain balance. This is seen by the positions of Venus in Pisces and her Libra ascendant, which are passive in energy and enjoy the free-flowing nature of harmony, peace and love. Smith has been described in the following way: "She seems to have been a rather sweet person; it does not appear that she ever harmed anybody or even harboured malevolent thoughts towards anyone" (Decker & Dummett, 2002, 131). When she lived at Bencoolen House, she used a local errand boy, Tony Edwards, who worked for the local grocer. He collected and delivered Smith's shopping for her as her health and mobility were deteriorating. He remembered her as being "pleasant and chatty" (Robinson, 2016, 48).

Mars is in Taurus in Smith's natal chart and suggests that when she did express her anger, she could be hot-tempered and obstinate. However, for some of the time she kept her fury and passion hidden. This is revealed by the position of Mars being situated in the eighth house. This is the area connected with the hidden and veiled (by way of it being associated with Scorpio and Pluto) where feelings are buried and concealed. Perhaps she had been raised with the premise, 'if you haven't got anything pleasant to say then say nothing at all,' which certainly is in keeping with the accommodating and sweet-natured quality of Venus – the ruler of her ascendant sign Libra (and Taurus). The ascendant is the area which governs our image and persona, the first impression we give to people and the qualities we project to other people.

So, whilst she may have *appeared* to have been sweet person, as portrayed in the aforementioned quote, she could also hide feelings of displeasure. Unfairness and unjustness are areas that Librans loathe and which particularly angered her. One example of this, as we have already seen, is with her constant battle with her publishers in getting her royalties and other payments she was owed from other parties.

The theme of privacy is extended by the Sun square Pluto aspect, which suggests that she went to great pains to hide some areas of herself. What remained private may have included her true feelings, as well as her psychic energy, which manifested through areas such as hunches and intuition. This aspect also shows that she was a survivor, had great inner strength and was a powerful and magnetic presence. One obvious example of her surviving a crisis and being able to move forward with her life was at the age of 21 when she became an orphan.

REALISM AND RESTLESSNESS, MAKING CHANGES AND WORKING HARD

The timing of this would have coincided around the time of her second transiting Saturn square natal Saturn and where Smith had to learn how to make her own way in the world and carve out a new life for herself. She had no rich parents, no husband to keep her (as was the norm then for the middle classes); neither did she have any siblings or immediate family to grieve with. This critical point in her life shows the Saturn energy and qualities at work by way of finality, identity and maturity. The Saturn lesson would have provoked her to become more realistic as well as becoming a more spiritual being.

Although she had no brothers or sisters; she was, however, close to a particular cousin in Jamaica, Mary Bidlack Reed, whom she regularly wrote to. She would often tell Reed about her art and the people she had met. Up until his death, Smith was still very close to her Uncle Theodore who on occasion visited his niece at her studio when she was performing her *Annancy Stories* (Kaplan, 2018, 151). Another example of her endurance and survival is surviving the two world wars – not everybody did.

Pluto is making other aspects in the natal chart, which comprises of Jupiter trine Pluto, Uranus square Pluto and Saturn sextile Pluto. Because the latter planet Pluto is in the eighth house (its associated position in the natural zodiac), it emphasises the forceful and powerful qualities brought to Smith's personality. Uranus square Pluto suggests that she took a pioneering approach to life and could initiate change in her life, which she most certainly did. One example being when she was in her early forties, by removing herself from her busy London life to one of contrasting social isolation when she relocated to Cornwall for the remainder of her life.

As we know, when she was a younger person, she travelled frequently overseas and back to England. In many ways, the energy of this aspect could have helped her to become easily accustomed to new things and any erratic events which may have been going on around her; such is the restless and unpredictable nature of Uranus. She may not necessarily have liked the drastic changes in her life; especially as Uranus and Pluto are governed by the fixed mode (which is associated with being immovable), but she was at least prepared for the unexpected and had the inner strength to make the changes she was forced to.

The Saturn sextile Pluto aspect also suggests lessons in survival and this was certainly true whereby Smith lived through the chauvinistic Victorian reign and later two other monarchs. Women were still expected to marry and have children and they were thought odd and unconventional if they did not adhere to the deep-rooted norms of society. However, Smith contributed to help make changes to the bigoted and classist culture through her work for the suffragette movement.

Jupiter trine Pluto also denotes a strong urge to reform in areas such as politics. Author and scholar, Elizabeth (Foley)

O'Connor, found that Smith "was also involved in other suffrage activities. Her name was included on a published Roll of Honour of women arrested for participating in suffrage protests and embroidered on a sash with other women who had spent at least one night in Royal Holloway Prison" (www.lostmodernists.com/pamela-colman-smith). Through this example, we can see how passionate Smith was about helping to change any hypocrisies and inequalities between the genders. It also shows her willingness to participate in suffrage activities, irrespective of the consequences showing her courage and drive.

Interestingly, on 11th January, 1910, Smith's name appeared in the Irish newspaper, *The Northern Whig* – the page was headlined: 'For and About Women.' Her name was included in an article about an arts and crafts exhibition which was in its ninth year, and where Walter Crane (the president of the society) wrote a foreword in the exhibition catalogue. It was a résumé of the organisation's history. Smith was exhibiting two watercolour paintings there: The *Snow is Dancing* and *The Coming of Spring*.

On the same page as the article, there is an editorial headlined: 'Suffragette's Claim for Damages.' It was about Emily Wilding Davison of the Women's Social and Political Union (WSPU) claiming for damages after being assaulted by prison officers whilst she was on hunger-strike in Strangeways Prison in Manchester. Later, and sadly, Davison became better-known for her death under the hooves of the King's horse on Derby Day in 1913. She and hundreds of other suffragettes sacrificed much in the struggle which eventually led to the successful campaign 'Votes for Women'.

On a personal level, Smith learnt about responsibilities when she had to help care for her mother and, towards the end of her life, Smith cared for her friend, Nora Lake, when she was ill. Also, as we already know, she had the responsibility of managing her father's estate in Jamaica after the death of her mother; duties included managing money by having to pay his employees.

The Moon quincunx Saturn aspect in her natal chart suggests that she may have felt "burdened by having to take care of sick or elderly family members" (Sakoian & Acker, 1972, 18). Being head of the large Parc Garland, which employed staff and hosted visiting priests to the property, was also a role where she had to be organised and sensible. In addition to this, other responsibility was held in her role as the sacristan for the chapel where she was accountable for items such as liturgical books and sacred vessels.

Saturn is in the sixth house (the area of health, co-workers/work and service) and indicates that she took her responsibilities seriously and worked hard for her money. She undertook collaborations and worked with co-workers, which would have appealed to her Libra ascendant. This is because this sign is associated with partnerships. It also suggests that as well as group situations, Smith enjoyed one-to-one working where ideas could be shared and where qualities of consideration and cooperation applied in the partnership (areas also associated with Libra). Her collaborations included working with Bram Stoker, Ellen Terry and, of course, her most famous one was with A.E. Waite.

The theme of her conscientious and industrious nature is echoed by Jupiter in Capricorn, which shows that she was driven, enjoyed working and was optimistic in her approach to employment and work. There is also a practical nature to Smith which is indicated in her natal chart by Mars in Taurus, which suggests that she was focused and hardworking and preferred not to waste time on frivolous pursuits if she had business and work tasks to undertake.

Ellen Terry wrote a letter to her son the actor and modern theatre practitioner, Edward Gordon Craig. She used Smith as an example as to how he might better manage his career and not waste his talents. Terry wrote: "She is extraordinarily industrious ... & is everlastingly making (& selling as fast as she makes) lamp shades, candle shades. Paints wee boxes, cards a dozen a day – trots them around. A funny little creature" (Holroyd, 2009, 452).

Here we can see how Smith liked to be busy and create whenever possible. Essentially, she had to keep creating, for she needed to earn money from this source as she was not in a privileged position of having wealthy parents to rely upon.

Terry wrote to her son about her: "This girl Pamela has quite wonderful business instincts & she is a really good sort…She is the sharpest little creature I have ever met" (Cockin, 2013, 4). It is possible that Smith may have accrued a little of her father's nous for business as he had been a merchant and businessman. However, a life of being a female artist was never going to be financially prosperous for her, given the patriarchal society she was living in; one wonders how much has changed for female artists since that time, if indeed it has at all.

Mars sextile the MC (*see glossary*) shows that Smith was brave and self-confident with a robust sense of self and a strong will to succeed in her career. When she was approximately 21 years old, John Butler Yeats said of her: "She will go far … because she believes in all her ideas … she has the simplicity and naiveté of an old dry-as-dust savant but with a child's heart" (Greer, 1995, 406) – thus recognising her self-belief, albeit in a back-handed compliment. Venus is trine the MC, which signals that Smith could excel in career fields such as the arts, design and fashion. It also indicates that her charisma would have helped her craft public presentational style, coupled with creativity and flair. This we know to have been true in the numerous and vivid descriptions of her appearance when she was storytelling, as well as her detailed and exemplary stage-costume designs.

RECOGNITION, DILIGENCE, ENVIRONMENT AND THE RIDER-WAITE TAROT DECK

Jupiter is considered a beneficiary planet and so, potentially, can bring fame and fortune; whilst Capricorn is associated with business and diligence. It is fitting therefore that Smith was finally

PAMELA COLMAN SMITH 1878–1951

27 AUG 1941

ROYAL SOCIETY OF ARTS
John Street, Adelphi, London, W.C.2

FOUNDED IN 1754 INCORPORATED BY ROYAL CHARTER IN 1847

PATRON: HIS MAJESTY THE KING

FORM OF PROPOSAL FOR FELLOWSHIP

Name in full *Corinne Pamela Mary Colman Smith* : 2.3

Address *"Gorseland," Upton Cliff, Bude, Cornwall.*

Rank, Profession or Business: *Artist • Illustrator – Teller of Folk Stories from Jamaica.*

I desire to become a Fellow of the Royal Society of Arts.

Signature of Candidate *Pamela Colman Smith*

We hereby propose and recommend the above Candidate as a fit and proper person to become a Fellow of the Royal Society for the Encouragement of Arts, Manufactures and Commerce.

Signatures of three Fellows, one of whom at least must sign on personal knowledge; or the nomination by the Council.

BY COUNCIL

PAID

Read and suspended

Elected **13 OCT 1941**

Cheques should be drawn to the order of the Royal Society of Arts and crossed "Coutts & Co." The annual subscription is £3 3s.; the life composition fee £31 10s. Overseas Fellows are requested to remit by a draft on their Bank in London, by International Money Order, or British Postal Orders.

PCS's Form for Proposal of Fellowship, with kind permission from the Royal Society of Arts.

awarded with the adequate credit and respect that she deserved some 100 years later, when the *Smith-Waite Centenarian Tarot Deck* was published and where her tremendous contribution was recognised and not overshadowed by A.E. Waite. Previously, in 1941, she was made a Fellow of the Royal Society of Arts (Royal Society of Arts, Manufactures and Commerce). She was elected under her full name of Corrine Pamela Mary Colman.

Edith Craig by Lena Connell, 1910.
www.commons.wikimedia.org – public domain.

She was proposed by council and her occupation was listed as artist, illustrator and teller of folk stories from Jamaica. She was immensely proud of her fellowship and from then regularly wrote the initials 'FRSA' on the back of her work.

In 2018, the beautiful and brilliantly researched *Pamela Colman Smith: The Untold Story* by Stuart R. Kaplan (with four scholars) was published and where much of her 'untold story' was finally revealed. Then, in 2021, Elizabeth Foley O'Connor's *Pamela Colman Smith: Artist, Feminist & Mystic* was published. More recently, other well-researched and inspiring books include: *Pamela Colman Smith – Tarot Artist – The Pious Pixie* by Dawn G. Robinson; *Secrets of The Waite-Smith Tarot* by Marcus Katz & Tali Goodwin; *The Queen of Wands* by Cat Willett; and the fictional *Magician and Fool* by Susan Wands. Clearly, Smith has made a significant resurgence and is rightly recognised and respected for the work that she did.

The sixth house is also associated with detailed work by its association with Virgo, which is the ruler of the sixth house in the natural zodiac. Saturn in this area suggests that Smith was

Lower Camden area in Chislehurst, the area where Pamela Colman Smith and her parents lived for a short while in approximately 1879/80. Photo reproduced by kind permission of Bromley Historic Collections.

talented at working with detail and specifications needed in her work. This is borne out by her illustrative work in the tarot deck and other various books, as well as a multitude of miniature toy theatres that she made. The detail in her work is also seen through her creations and designs of the players, set designs and stage costumes. Other careful and detailed work of hers can be seen in the *Green Sheaf* publication, where each copy had been hand-coloured and a green bow embroidered on the reverse of it (Katz & Goodwin, 2020).

Smith spent some of her time at Smallhythe with Ellen Terry and her family whilst she was designing the tarot. The environment, landscapes and people there inspired some of her designs. For example, the Queen of Wands card is believed to have been modeled on Edith (Edy) Craig with her cat, Snuffles (Katz & Goodwin, 2020, 231).

When she was creating the tarot deck for A.E. Waite (also a passionate astrologer), he instructed Smith to "follow very carefully the astrological significance of each suit as it is influenced by different zodiacal signs" (www.holisticshop.co.uk).

Wands 13, 'Rider-Waite Tarot Deck'. Queen of Wands Tarot Card. www.commons.wikimedia.org – public domain.

Nine of Swords, 'Waite-Smith Tarot Deck'. Yale University. www.commons.wikimedia.org – public domain.

The Emperor Tarot Card, RWS. Tarot 4 Emperor. www.commons.wikimedia.org – public domain.

The Star Tarot Card. www.commons.wikimedia.org – public domain RWS – Tarot 17 Star Published in 1909.

The Strength Tarot Card – RWS Tarot 08 – Strength – Published in 1909.

Following his request, Smith symbolised the suits as follows: wands for fire, pentacles for earth, swords for air and cups for water. This shows Smith's detailed astrological artwork. There is representation of the elements, zodiac signs and planetary symbolism virtually everywhere in the cards.

One example of this can be seen in the Nine of Swords card. Looking closely at the patchwork cover on the person's bed, one can see astrological and planetary glyphs in the design. The Major Arcana are represented by each of the zodiac signs too, the Aries card shows the Emperor in red attire showing the hue of Mars – the ruling planet of Aries and the colour representing the fire element. The sign is symbolised by the ram and four rams' heads can be seen on the Emperor's throne.

The remaining zodiac signs are represented in the Major Arcana by the following: Hierophant/Taurus, Lovers/Gemini, Chariot/Cancer, Strength/Leo, Hermit/Virgo, Justice/Libra, Death/Scorpio, Temperance/Sagittarius, Devil/Capricorn/, Aquarius/Star, Moon/Pisces. Smith's Sun sign is represented by the Star card and her Moon sign by the Strength card.

Natural settings provide the environment and backdrop for each of Smith's Minor Arcana cards (and other additional artworks) with visible signs of the elements in her artwork, and it is evident how she had a passion for the beauty of nature. As a very young child, she was inspired by the natural world and scenery around her. Although she lived at Chislehurst when she was just a tot, the environment clearly had an impact on her.

When she was in her early twenties, she wrote to her friend, author Albert Bigelow Paine, that Chislehurst had "lovely woods and clouds of bluebells" (Kaplan, 2018, 356). It is possible that she returned to visit the area when she was older, perhaps on her way to Smallhythe. It would have been manageable to travel from London to Kent to visit both Chislehurst and Smallhythe.

The Chislehurst Caves, which are near to where she lived in Lower Camden, opened to the public in 1900 (www.chislehurst-

ASTROLOGY SECOND SIGHT ART

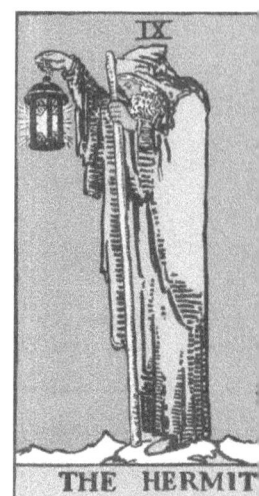

(*left*) Druid figure from the Druids Section in the Chislehurst Caves. Photograph copyright of Chislehurst Caves (Kent Mushroom Ltd.).
(*right*) The Hermit Tarot Card. www.commons.wikimedia.org – public domain. RWS Tarot 09 – The Hermit – published in 1909.

caves.co.uk/#about), before the tarot deck was released. If Smith had visited the caves, she may have been inspired by the area and the figures and etchings that were done in the caves throughout its long history. She may have used any stimulation that she had from her visit there later in some of her images for the cards in the tarot deck. For example, there is an area within the Druids section of the caves where a figure mildly resembles The Hermit card in the tarot deck. This is all speculation however.

Perhaps the experience of living near such beautiful surroundings remained with her and was why she enjoyed visiting Smallhythe in Kent and the West Country (Cornwall, Devon and Somerset, including Glastonbury). It may of course have been a welcome break for her in being able to escape from city life.

Returning again to the astrology; in 1904, she wrote again to Paine and by this time she was involved in the Hermetic Order of the Golden Dawn. It appears the subject of astrology appealed to the mystical and pragmatic side of her nature. She asked Paine in her letter: "Do you know anything of astrology? It seems to me more practical than most other things" (Robinson, 2020, 26). During June of 1916, Smith took part in the art tent at a Temple of Mystery bazaar that provided "high class astrology and demonology" (Kaplan & Boyd Parsons, 2018, 84).

RESPONSIBILITY, SACRIFICE, AWARENESS AND FUNDRAISING

Saturn and Venus are in Pisces in her natal chart, which indicates that Smith could be very compassionate and enjoyed helping those less fortunate than herself, which she would have found rewarding. One aforementioned example of this is when she assumed the role of carer for her mother and Nora Lake. She also created a poster for the Polish Victim's Relief Fund during the First World War in 1915 (Kaplan, 2018, 85), and she hosted bazaars in her flat and then gave the proceeds to the Red Cross and other groups (ibid). During the First World War, she intermittently continued storytelling and in 1917 she appeared at the Savoy Hotel for a matinee performance which was in support of the Women Wartime Workers (Kaplan & Foley O'Connor, 2018, 84).

These examples show not only her benevolent and charitable nature, as indicated by the energy of Saturn and Venus in Pisces, but also how working for different groups was equally as satisfying for her, as were her collaborations. This is shown by the position of the Moon and Uranus in the eleventh house of her natal chart. She was involved with a wide variety of groups in her lifetime, which included the Catholic congregation of her church, the Hermetic Order of the Golden Dawn, the Irish Literacy Society, the Lyceum Theatre Company, the Masquers, the Pioneer Players, the Suffrage Atelier and the Women's Art Workers Guild.

This shows her embracing and sociable Aquarian nature, as well as a need to belong to a common cause. It also indicates that she needed to be stimulated and her skills and talents put to good use. One example of her work with the Suffrage Ateiler can be seen whereby she produced two identifiable postcards and she signed them as 'P.S. – unlike in her creative work where she usually signed with the familiar black caduceus – like symbol of PCS. The example of these two postcards by Smith present a contemptuous yet humorous angle on some of the deceit, injustices and obstacles that women were faced with when dealing with government and parliament as well as the attitude towards suffragettes by those in positions of power. One of the postcards is reproduced here.

Smith assisted with campaigning, fundraising and creative outputs to support group needs. Two examples of this are seen by her work for the Women's Suffrage Movement and also for the box-workers, whose trade was hit hard during the First World War (www.britishnewspaperarchive.co.uk). She created and designed a cardboard box cottage. It was described by *The Common Cause magazine as a* "delightful little house of cardboard with garden and trees" (ibid) and it was sold for one shilling. Her creation gave work to the struggling box-workers as well as a humble income for herself.

Archives show that Smith was imprisoned for one evening in Holloway Prison for Women in connection with her suffrage activities. Before the First World War, the prison was used to imprison suffragettes who broke the law. Other suffragettes imprisoned there included Emily Davison and Emmeline Pankhurst. Scholar, Elizabeth (Foley) O'Connor, believes that "the involvement in the suffrage movement played a key role in the development of Colman Smith's feminist consciousness and the evolution of her symbolic depiction of women" (www.lostmodernists.com/pamela-colman-smith).

In November 1912, *The Common Cause* weekly publication, which supported the National Union of Women's Suffrage Societies, reported that the International Suffrage Shop held a fundraising event. Smith was there with a stall selling Christmas cards and hand-coloured prints as well as showing calendars

Suffragette postcard drawn by PCS/PS – 'A Bird in the Hand is Worth Two in the Bush.' Reproduced with permission of the Women's Library at the London School of Economics.

(www.britishnewspaperarchive.co.uk). The International Suffrage Shop has been described as "the only feminist bookshop" (www.womanandhersphere.com).

The *Daily Mirror* (reporter unknown) commented in November of 1903 on Smith's artwork and the venue of the exhibition where she along with artist, Cecil French, were showcasing their work at a small gallery in Bayswater, London. The article in the newspaper was headed *'Dreams and Visions'* and it read: "At an exhibition in Bayswater in a little gallery which has been turned into a mystical dreamland by the brush and pencil of two artists – Miss Pamela Colman Smith and Mr Cecil French. Miss Colman Smith is the more sympathetic," it continued, "the appeal of her 'Dream Pictures' and 'Waking Visions' is more direct because she makes us feel her own sincerity. They are visions which have obviously been actually seen by an ingenious mind from which the fairyland glimpses of childhood have not been affected by the contact with a stern world" (*Daily Mirror*, 1903, 6).

This shows how she was able to convey through paintings her fertile imagination as well as her observations from the spirit realms. Clearly, the newspaper reporter was stirred by the magic of her artwork. By turning the exhibition space into a "mystic dreamland" the artists had given thought to their audience, providing a total experience for them.

In 1903, Smith was described by a newspaper reporter as having "delighted the children in attendance," referring to her performance of storytelling. This was after her public appearance for a Christmas Hans Andersen bazaar in London which was held to support the Girls Realm Guild of Service (Kaplan & Foley O'Connor, 2018, 70). This again shows Smith's communication skills at being able to hold the attention of her audience in an enchanting and entertaining way. By seating herself on the floor when she was storytelling, she was in effect coming to their level, implying that they were all equal.

ENTERTAINMENT AND HOSPITALITY

The author of the 1930s book series *Swallows and Amazons*, Arthur Ransome (cousin to Christabel Marshall, Edith Craig's partner), described in his book, *Bohemia in London*, how when he was approximately nineteen years old, he paid his first visit to Smith's studio for a soirée of her entertainment. He described how "She welcomed us with a little shriek, half laugh half exclamation … Just now at the door they were the eyes of a joyous excited child meeting the guests of a birthday party" (Ransome, 1984, 54), which indicates her affectionate and childlike ways.

Ransome described her and the setting of the studio in great detail. Turning to his friend as they approached Smith's residence, he told his companion: "Her name is Gypsy … No one ever calls her anything else" (ibid). As the two excitedly approached her front door, Ransome glimpsed through a window and he saw "a silver lamp, and a brazen candlestick, and a weird room in

PCS reciting a folktale, 1907.
www.commons.wikimedia.org – public domain.

shaded lamplight" (ibid). He went on to describe how the front door was flung open and they saw "a little round woman, scarcely more than a girl, standing at the threshold. She was dressed in an orange-coloured coat that hung loose over a green skirt, with black tassels sewn all over the orange silk, like the frills on a red Indian's trousers" (ibid). Clearly, she had a sense of colour, drama and style. He continued to describe her: "She was very dark and not thin and when she smiled, with a smile that was peculiarly infectious, her twinkling gypsy eyes seemed to vanish altogether" (ibid).

Ransom was obviously taken with Smith's warmth, as well as her distinct and mesmerising presence. His enthusiasm was heightened as she shuffled down the hallway and led them into "a mad room out of a fairytale … it had the effect of a well-designed curiosity shop … the walls were dark green and covered with brilliant coloured drawings, etchings and pastel sketches" (Ransome, 1984, 55).

Before Smith commenced her performances for her guests, she offered them her specialty drink which was 'Opal Hush' – red claret with lemonade (Ransome, 1984, 58). The evening continued and Smith took her place, ready to perform. She sat "in a high-backed chair that was covered with gold and purple embroideries ... leant forward so that the lamplight fell on her weird little face" (ibid) and sang an old melody.

She continued the entertainment by also reciting a poem of Yeats', *Wind among the Reeds*, as well as singing an old sea shanty and finally by telling folktales, which were the *Annancy Stories* – told in Jamaican patois. One character included in the tales was that of the Obeah Woman who was a witch "wid winkles deep as ditches on her brown face" (Ransome, 1984, 61). The Obeah women were found in the former British colonies of the Caribbean and were essential figures in communities. They practiced healing, using animal and herbal ingredients, and they also practiced spell craft.

The aforementioned experience described by Ransome perfectly illustrates the 'astrology in action' – i.e. the Moon in Leo position. We can see her generosity of spirit, hospitality, creativity and sense of occasion, as well as the pleasure it gave her in seeing her friends enjoy themselves and where she was both hostess and entertainer with an adoring audience.

Ransome was greatly inspired by Smith and held her storytelling talent in high esteem. In his autobiography, he wrote that for ten years he had been repeating to friends and their children the Jamaican stories that he had heard from 'Pixie' Colman Smith (Hart-Davis, 1976, 157). He also wrote that after his first visit to her studio he "was soon one of the fortunate ones with a permanent invitation." Smith was obviously fond of him and enjoyed his company (Hart-Davis, 1976, 87).

He recalled how it was at Smith's studio that he met for the first time the poet, W.B. Yeats, and that sometimes actress, Ellen Terry, was there. Ransome declared that Smith read

Yeats' poetry so well that 50 years later, he could not read them to himself "without hearing her read them to me" (ibid). It has also been observed that Smith was well known for her chanting performances of Yeats' poetry. She was close to the Yeats family and W.B. Yeats' father once described her as "a savant with a child's heart" (Holroyd, 2009, 452).

Smith also designed costumes and was hands-on for productions and particularly for matinée performances, which were often scheduled for children. One example of this can be seen whereby in the Easter Holidays of 1914, a stage version of Uncle Remus' *Brer Rabbit and Mr. Fox* was shown at the Little Theatre in Hampstead. Smith was credited in the local newspaper as having "designed the dresses and properties" (*Hampstead and St. John's Advertiser*, 1914, 5). The publication, *The Gentlewoman*, reported in 1904 that Smith was part of an ensemble of artists that were performing in the Café Chantant for the Princess Christian Infant Nursery in Windsor at the Victoria Hall White Hart Hotel, between 3.30pm-6.30pm.

Princess Christian was a daughter of Queen Victoria and patron of the nursery and she was fundraising for the nursery through the event. The organisation eventually became known as HRH Princess Christian's Training College and Infant Nursery, it accommodated 32 babies and the home was largely supported by the Children's Union. Originally, it was set up in the 1870s as the Home for Babies in Windsor to provide working mothers with a safe place to leave their babies whilst they were at work (www.hiddenlives.org.uk/homes).

The report in *The Gentlewoman* also wrote that Smith had "recently appeared before the King at Sandringham" (*The Gentlewoman*, 1904, 5), inferring that her billing at Windsor was a privileged one. For a good while Smith enjoyed performing, although this ceased when she was in her early to mid-thirties.

Before she grew dissatisfied with performing for her audiences and was still entertaining, in one edition of the *Green Sheaf* she advertised the services of Gelukiezanger: teller of West Indian folktales at entertainments. Of course, 'Gelukiezanger' was in fact Smith. "For this role she dressed in voluminous, barbaric robes of red and orange with coral and amber beads twined in her hair" (Waite, 1995, xiv).

The description continued. "Her slanting Chinese eyes and dark-skinned full face added to the effect" (ibid). Smith had a stage manager to assist her too; a man-servant would bring in a small folding platform and set it up for her, with a few candles in front to light up her face in the darkened room. Once the preparation had been carried out, Gelukiezanger would sit cross-legged on the platform and begin her storytelling (ibid). This shows how Smith took her storytelling seriously by creating a persona with a colourful and dramatic costume, using a stage manager to help with props and using lighting for maximum effect to help create the atmosphere and mood that she required in an intimate theatrical setting for her storytelling.

PURPOSE AND SPIRITUAL FULFILMENT

In astrology, the Moon's Nodes are the symbolic point in the sky where the paths of the Moon and Sun cross. They are considered karmic points which are believed to give you guidance on how to live your life in order to advance on your spiritual path. The North Node indicates the qualities one should develop, whilst the South Node indicates ones that should be inhibited. They also provide answers and insight to deeper and philosophical questions such as *'what is the purpose of my life'* and *'why am I here?'*

Smith's North Node was in Aquarius and her South Node in Leo in the fifth and eleventh house respectively, so what does this mean about Smith's vocation in life? Astrologer and author, Victor Olliver, using the draconic (*see glossary*) method of astrology observed the following: People with this node pairing have "immense talent and energies can be dedicated to a personal passion, but life will draw you into collective activity where broader, impersonal or humanitarian causes or objectives benefit from your drive" (Olliver, 2022, 48). This is pertinent to Smith and what we know of her life. As a young child, she had a passion for art and drawing which developed and progressed when she was an older teenager and continued throughout adulthood.

She used her artistic and practical skills for groups such as theatre companies, the suffragette movement and various charities, as well as the tarot-using community by setting an accessible template for future tarot decks. When she relocated to Cornwall, she tried her best to continue the running of the small Catholic mission already there. This was done by her offering a place of worship on her land for the tiny Catholic community at The Lizard.

This shows the collective activity and broader humanitarian causes and objectives of the North Node and Sun positioned in Aquarius. It shows that indeed Smith did achieve her life's purpose and, as we have already seen, there were several challenges in her life whilst she endeavoured to achieve her intentions and objectives.

Her friends, commentators, researchers and writers were (and remain) baffled as to why Smith converted to Catholicism and moved away from her busy social life in London. Astrology offers some of the answers. On 7th April, 1914, when she wrote in her bursting visitor's book that she'd had enough of people, there were some transiting planets in her natal chart which provide insight and significant information.

It shows that on the aforementioned date in 1914, her Sun had progressed (*see glossary under 'Progressions'*) into Aries, the ascendant had progressed into Scorpio, whist the MC had progressed into Leo and the progressed Moon was in Sagittarius. This shows that she was searching for a new start in life, was feeling inspired and was looking for a new direction where she could have more freedom and direct her own path (more so than previously) and where her new found values could be put into place. This was approximately four years before she finally moved to Cornwall.

Transiting Pluto (one of the planets associated with beginnings and endings) was in Smith's ninth house on the aforementioned date. This is the area associated with beliefs, meaning, religion, morality, principles and freedom. It suggests that her spiritual journey would be transformed and could bring new religious experiences which potentially could help her grow. The urge to spread her wings would have been powerful, as would the draw for adventures, new places and new people. She converted to Catholicism in 1911, but had been involved in helping the Catholic Church previously to this. By 1914, her desire for something even more spiritually meaningful was evident. Then, in 1918/1919, she was living in a new area, owned her own property and land, as well as running the small Catholic mission on her estate. This was a total transformation and rebirth in her life and from this we can see the qualities of transiting Pluto in the ninth house at work.

CLOSING THE CIRCLE

By the time Smith died in 1951, there were several major astrological transits occurring, mainly concerned with transiting Mars and Pluto at the eleventh house, although there were others too. Transiting Saturn was in the twelfth house and indicates that Smith was withdrawing from life, perhaps even experiencing a reduction in confidence too, as well as spending more time alone than in her previous years. Saturn is associated with austerity, decay, old age and wisdom, as well as fear and limitations.

Smith was living with financial limitations and austerity unlike ever before and now living in a flat in Bude. Every week, she would telephone the local grocery shop to give a very modest order. In addition, she asked for a milk loaf from the bakery opposite (Robinson, 2020, 178/179). Her goods would be delivered to the lobby of her flat where there were many drawings and sketches (Robinson, 2020, 179). Apparently, she accounted for every penny when paying her grocery bill (Robinson, 2020, 182), illustrating how aware she was of her restricted finances.

The manifestation of Saturn at the twelfth house is seen by some of the information that (as previously discussed) Tony Edwards shared with author, Dawn G. Robinson. In 1943, and when Smith was approximately 65 years old, he recalled from those times the following. Smith was "not exactly slim, and was grey around the temples, with her hair swept back in a bun" (Robinson, 2020, 178) and "I used to have to go to the chemist … to collect her thermal wadding and her medications" (Robinson, 2020, 181). It was obvious that Smith "had her aches and pains, quite likely from the bad chest that indicated later heart problems" (Robinson, 2020, 179). It has been said of Smith that "she was a kind-hearted woman who appreciated his services" (ibid), '*his*' being Tony Edwards.

Fortunately, in later years, Smith had some assistance from her "friend and neighbour, Elsie T. Bates who occasionally helped the largely bed-bound Pamela with cleaning and other household tasks" (Kaplan & Foley O' Connor, 2018, 90). Smith was living with myocardial degeneration. Some of the symptoms of this include swelling in the legs, ankles and feet, shortness of breath with activity, reduced ability to exercise, as well as very rapid weight gain from fluid retention (www.mayoclinic.org). These warning signs were probably contributing factors as to how Smith became bed-bound.

Presumably, by this time, Nora Lake had also become frail and infirm, although (as we know) she outlived Smith. Lake died in 1962 in a nursing home in Exeter. Smith's friend Elsie found her dead in bed on 18th September, 1951 (Kaplan & Foley O' Connor, 2018, 90), which must have been shocking and upsetting for her.

Transiting Mars was conjunct Smith's natal Moon when she died. This suggests that Smith may have been feeling more irritable and snappier, which is understandable if she was in pain and discomfort. Close friends may have been the target of her anger – which may well have been Bates or Lake.

Transiting Mars square natal Pluto also indicates a time of fierce power struggles and disagreements and that Smith may have had to deal with challenges to her ego. The transiting Uranus on the MC/tenth house suggests that she could also have been restless and unpredictable, even aloof. If this was true, it appears that it was with the people close to her and given that (as best as we know) she was only close to Lake and Bates at the end of her life, it will have been these two women who were subject to Smith's agitation and tension.

Transiting Pluto was also conjunct her natal Moon, this indicates that she may have felt that she no longer had any control over her life or home because she was dependent on others. This may also have brought back repressed feelings from the past when she cared for her mother before she died. Those feelings may have been intense and resentful as they are qualities associated with Pluto. Naturally, she would have probably considered her own mortality as her health increasingly faded and, as we know, Pluto is associated with death and transformation.

Relationships with women may also have been more intense, and/or acute power struggles may have ensued – especially if Smith felt that a person was trying to run her life for her. Whether this was the case between her and Nora Lake, we do not know. The transiting Pluto square natal Pluto reveals that complex and profound changes were inevitable at this period of her life. Certainly, transformation was underway by both a metaphysical and physical death.

Transiting Mars and Pluto were in the eleventh house when Smith died. This indicates that there had been great changes in her life by that time and that any long-term plans for her future may have changed. One example being that she had to hand back the chapel to the diocese which she had fought hard for and probably thought she would be at Parc Garland until her dying days.

Her change of ideals may have been reflected in the people she associated with and this can be seen by most of her London friends moving away from her when she converted to Catholicism. Equally, it could be said that it was Smith undergoing a transformation, and so was moving away from them.

Any friends that she did have in her last few years had a purpose to them and she no longer had the many casual encounters or shallow old friendships that she previously had. Living in an isolated and remote area would have helped put pay to that. Under the Mars and Pluto transits, we can see that Smith underwent a transformation of both her friendships and a regeneration of her goals.

On the day that Smith died, her progressions chart shows that the Sun had progressed into Taurus, the ascendant was in Scorpio and the MC was in Virgo. This suggests that leading up to that time, Smith may have become obstinate, wilful and bolshie, as well as critical and sensitive. If this was true of her then it would have tested even the most patient of carers and friends. These qualities of course may have been a mask and distraction from any fears she may have had about death and dying.

She outlived her parents' ages when she died aged 73. Her life was one full of artistry, spirituality and variety. Often on the margins, she defied society's convention of what was expected of a woman from her background and class. She was driven by her passion for art and creativity and was believed to still be creating art in her perennial years. She was incensed by inequalities and campaigned for those who had no voice and who were treated unfairly. She had a rich inner life and was on a spiritual path to making a difference to humanity through collective activities.

Her given names of 'Corrine Pamela' are relevant to Smith by definition. The name Corrine is thought to be French and Greek in origin and means 'beautiful maiden' and 'spear' – thus symbolising a female warrior who has great beauty and strength (www.en.wikipedia.org/wiki). The name Pamela is believed to have been invented in the sixteenth century by poet, Sir Philip Sidney, and translates to 'honey' or 'all sweetness'. Pamela was a key character in his prose, *The Countess of Pembroke's Arcadia* (ibid).

Little could Corrine Pamela Mary Colman Smith have known how influential her artwork for the *Rider-Waite Tarot Deck* would be, especially after her death and how it stimulated many tarot-readers and sitters as well as designers for other tarot decks. Her other artwork has brought joy to many art-lovers and can be seen in various libraries and institutions. Her participation in campaign work for the suffragette movement helped towards eventually reform, votes and other rights for women.

It is no wonder that the futuristic Corrine Pamela Mary Colman Smith is still with us in different ways and is currently experiencing resurgence. The independent, unique and rebellious Aquarius that she was remained true to herself, shining her star and pouring new water on to staid and old ground.

ACKNOWLEDGMENTS, CREDITS AND REFERENCES

THANKS TO:

Assistant Archivist at the Royal Society of Arts (Royal Society for Arts Manufactures & Commerce), for information and images on Smith's FRSA application form.

Astrodienst, for their website www.astro.com enabling natal and transits charts to be generated.

Bromley Historic Collections – the Archives Assistant – for information on the Smith and Ward families in Chislehurst as well as accessing the photograph of Lower Camden for use in publishing.

City of Westminster – the Archives Assistant for information on the tenants and residents at 27 Belgravia Road in 1878.

Elizabeth Crawford, author of *Art and Suffrage: A Biographical Dictionary of Suffrage Artists*, for directing me to www.lostmodernists.com website.

Katharine Cockin, for suggesting particular references and sources regarding Corrine Pamela Colman Smith.

Manchester Archives & Local History Service, for information from the 1881 Census re the Smith family in Didsbury.

Mary K. Greer, for permission to reformat the photograph of Pamela Colman Smith, taken by photographer, Alice Boughton (which appears on www.marykgreer.com website) for use in this book.

Phil Hodges, for permission to use the image of Parc Garland and the Catholic church which was formerly at The Lizard.

Susannah Mayor, archivist for the National Trust at Smallhythe Place, for her passion for Pamela Colman Smith and interest in the Colman Smith chapter of this book, as well her willingness in sharing her thoughts on perceived truths.

Dawn G. Robinson, for putting me in contact with Hayley White and assisting in other communications, as well as her generosity of spirit.

Royal Shakespeare Company - Images Manager, for notation information on reverse of photo showing Pamela Colman Smith et al outside Anne Hathaway's cottage.

Hayley White, for the postcard of the Catholic church formerly at The Lizard, and also of her encouragement for this book and her passion for Pamela Colman Smith.

ASTROLOGY DETAIL

Natal chart generated by www.astro.com (Astrodienst).

Rodden Rating Classification is 'X' for the natal chart based on rectification method.

Smith Colman, P. Saturday 16th February, 1878, at 21.00pm (rectified), Pimlico, London (formerly Middlesex), U.K. Co-ordinates: 0w10, 51n30.

BLOG

Mary K. Greer's tarot blog:
Pamela Colman Smith: A New Pair of Eyes and Ears (27th February, 2018) – Accessed on 04/03/2023. https://marykgreer.com/2018/02/27/pamela-colman-smith-a-new-pair-of-eyes-and-ears/

BOOKS

Clifford, F.C. (2012) *Getting to the Heart of your Chart: Playing Astrological Detective*. Flare Publications.

Hand Clow, B. (2007) *Rainbow Bridge – Between the Inner and Outer Planets*. Llewellyn Publications.

Cockin, K. (2013) *Collected Letters of Ellen Terry – Volume 4: 1899–1905*. Pickering & Chatto.

Cockin, K. (1998) *Edith Craig (1869–1947) – Dramatic Lives*. Cassell.

Cockin, K. (2001) *Women and Theatre in the Age of Suffrage – The Pioneer Players 1911–1925*. Palgrave.

Crawford, E. (2018) *Art and Suffrage: A Biographical Dictionary of Suffrage Artists*. Francis Boutle Publishers.

Croft, S. & Cockroft, I. (2010) *Art, Theatre and Women's Suffrage*. Aurora Metro Press.

Dummett, M. & Decker, R. (2013) *A History of the Occult Tarot*. Duckworth Overlook.

Greer, M. (1995) *Women of the Golden Dawn – Rebels and Priestesses*. Park Street Press.

Hart-Davis, R. (1976) prologue and epilogue for *The Autobiography of Arthur Ransome*. Jonathan Cape Ltd.

Holroyd, M. (2009) *A Strange Eventful History: The Dramatic Lives of Ellen Terry and Henry Irving*. Vintage Books.

Kaplan, Stuart R. with Mary K Greer, Elizabeth Foley O' Connor, Melinda Boyd Parsons (2018) *Pamela Colman Smith – The Untold Story*. U.S. Games Systems, Inc.

Katz, M. & Goodwin, T. (2020) *Secrets of the Waite-Smith Tarot*. Llewellyn Publications.

Olliver, V. (2022) *The Wessex Astrologer: 'Chasing the Dragons: An Introduction to Astrology.'*

Ransome, A. (1984) *Bohemia in London*. Oxford University Press.

Reinhart, M. (1989) *Chiron and the Healing Journey: An Astrological and Psychological Perspective*. Penguin Books.

Robinson, Dawn G. (2020) *Pamela Colman Smith –Tarot Artist – The Pious Pixie*. Fonthill Media Limited.

Robinson, Dawn G. (2016) *Secret Bude*. Amberley Publishing.

Smith Colman Smith, P. (2006) *Annancy Stories*. Darken Intentions Press.

Colman Smith, P. (2010) *Susan and the Mermaid*. Corrine Kenner.

Stoker, B. (1911) *Illustrated Lair of the White Worm*. Lightning Source UK Ltd.

Terry, E. (2017) *The Russian Ballet*. Okitoks Press.

Thomas, Z. (2020) *Women Art Workers and the Arts & Crafts Movement.* Manchester University Press.
Tompkins, S. (1990) *Aspects in Astrology: A Comprehensive Guide to Interpretation.* Element Books Limited.
Waite, A.E. (1995) *The Pictorial Key to the Tarot.* A Citadel Press Book published by Carol Publishing Group.
Waite, A.E. (2016) *Shadows of Life and Thought – The Autobiography of A.E. Waite.* Bardic Press.
Wands, S. (2017) *Magician and Fool.* i2i Publishing.
Willett, C. (2022) *The Queen of Wands – The Story of Pamela Colman Smith, the Artist Behind the Rider-Waite Tarot Deck.* Hachette Book Group.

MAGAZINES

The Common Cause (date unknown) from the British Newspaper Archives/ British Library, headline *'Toys'* – raising funds to help the box-workers whose trade had been hit hard.

NEWSPAPERS

The Cambria Daily Leader. Tuesday 16th June, 1908 – headline *'TOPICS OF THE TIMES'*.
The Daily Mirror. 18th November, 1903, page 6 (reporter unknown) – article headed *'The Allied Arts of Painting & Enameling'* – description of artwork at a gallery in Bayswater.
The Gentlewoman. 30th January, 1903, page 17 (reporter unknown) – article about Colman Smith appearing in an afternoon performance involving various artists in Windsor, at the White Hart Hotel at the Victoria Hall and noting that she had recently performed for the King (Edward VII) at Sandringham.
Hampstead and St. John's Wood Advertiser. Date unknown but thought to be approx. April, 1914, page 5 – article headlined *'Mrs Dearmer's Holiday Matinées'*.
The Northern Whig. Tuesday 11th January, 1910 (reporter un-named) – article about Emily Davison and her treatment in prison.
The Weekly Journal. Friday 12th April, 1907 (reporter un-named) – article headlined *'Story of the Poach Egg – It made Mark Twain Laugh'* – information about Colman Smith telling *Annancy Stories* in America.

PDF

The British Newspaper Archives: *The Weekly* Journal. Friday 12th April, 1907, page 15 – article on *'Story of "De Six Poach Eggs" – It Made Mark Twain Laugh'* (reporter unknown).

WEBSITES

https://artsandculture.google.com/asset/an-anti-suffrage-alphabet-book-housman-laurence/igF9dyIeRyd4lQ?hl=en – Detail about the book *An Anti-Suffragette Alphabet*. Accessed on 19/01/2023.

https://www.britishnewspaperarchive.org.uk – *The Standard* newspaper, edition no. 16, 716, Tuesday 19th February, 1878 – notices under Births, Marriages & Deaths – for the birth of a daughter to Corrine Colman & Charles E. Smith.

https://www.britishnewspaperarchive.org.uk – *The Common Cause* 14th November, 1912 – Smith selling her merchandise at The International Suffrage Shop. Accessed on 10/03/2023.

https://chislehurst-caves.co.uk/#about – Date for when the caves opened to the public. Accessed on 14/04/2023.

https://www.collinsdictionary.com/dictionary/english/diseuse – Definition of 'diseuse'. Accessed on 13/03/2023.

https://embrace-autism.com/autism-and-synesthesia – Information about some people with synesthesia being on the autistic spectrum. Accessed on 19/03/2023.

https://www.findagrave.com/memorial/205139046/corinne-smith – Information about Corrine "Serena" Colman Smith and her grave details along with additional family information and photograph. Accessed on 05/03/2023.

https://www.hiddenlives.org.uk/homes/WINDS02.html – Information about Princess Christian Infant Nursery. Accessed on 19/02/2023.

https://www.holisticshop.co.uk/articles/bio-of-arthur-edward-waite – The instructions A. E. Waite gave to Colman Smith to produce the tarot cards. Accessed on 31/01/2023.

https://jis.gov.jm/information/get-the-facts/origin-anancynancy-stories – Information on the origins and meaning of Anancy/Nancy stories. Accessed on 04/02/2023.

https://lostmodernists.com/pamela-colman-smith – Vol. 1, Issue 1, *Pamela Colman Smith: From Tarot Artist to Suffrage Activist* by Elizabeth O'Connor – information pertaining to Smith's work for the suffragettes and Suffrage Atelier. Accessed on 29/01/2023.

https://www.mayoclinic.org/diseases-conditions/heart-failure/symptoms-causes/syc-20373142 – Details of symptoms of myocardial degeneration. Accessed on 10/04/2022.

https://mystic.fandom.com/wiki/Golden_Dawn_Zelator – Golden Dawn and Zelator explanation. Accessed on 11/03/2023.

https://pcs2051.tripod.com/index.htm – Phil Norfleet on Smith's mother being a fan of English theatre. Accessed on 13/03/2023.

https://swedenborg.com/emanuel-swedenborg/influence – Swedenborg and spiritualism. Accessed on 28/03/2023.

https://uksynaesthesia.com – Description of what synaesthesia is. Accessed on 19/03/2023.

https://www.suffrageresources.org.uk/database/2276/mr-henry-wood-nevinson – Forgotten Champions – Henry Wood Nevinson's roles. Accessed on 11/03/2023.

https://en.wikipedia.org/wiki/Corinne_(name) – Definition of the name Corrine. Accessed on 11/03/2023.

https://en.wikipedia.org/wiki/Pamela_(name) – Definition of the name Pamela. Accessed on 11/03/2023.

https://womanandhersphere.com/2013/06/11/suffrage-stories-the-international-suffrage-shop – The nature of the International Suffrage Shop. Accessed on 10/03/2023.

CHAPTER TWO

Madge Gill 1882–1961

Mother and Wife, Outsider Artist and Medium

Madge Gill was an English 'Outsider Artist' and visionary. Her creative outpouring of mediumistic art began after the deaths of two of her children. She had a disjointed childhood and her life story was one of triumph over much adversity and pain.

BIOGRAPHY

Madge Gill was born on the 19th January, 1882, and died on the 28th January, 1961. She was born at 173 Marsh Street, Essex – which is now 65 High Street, Walthamstow, London. Her given name was Maud Eades. She was born to Emma Elizabeth Eades, who was nearly 28 years old when she gave birth to Maud, who was to be her only child. On Maud's birth certificate, the father is unnamed. However, his identity was apparently known to the Eades family and it has been said that "Madge's unidentified father was a source of shame within the family" (*LIGHT*, 2019, 12).

There is a theory about the identity of her father, which is that he could have been a portrait painter with the surname Sargent who lived in Blackheath (Cardinal, 1972, 135) – an area in Lewisham, South-East London. Emma was living with relatives in Lewisham when she became pregnant. The 1881 Census (just nine months before Maud's birth) shows that a Frederick Sargent was living with his widowed mother and siblings in Lee (near

Madge Gill at work, 19 August 1947. Getty Images: Photo by Russell Westwood/Popperfoto via Getty Images.

Lewisham). The Census shows that he was an engineer by trade (possibly he was also an artist). The same document shows that a 'visitor' to the Sargent family home was Emma Eades. This indicates that there was the opportunity for physical relations to take place between Emma and Frederick Sargent. He later married, and the 1911 Census (www.ancestry.co.uk/NRO) shows Emma's brother, Walter, as being a 'visitor' to the home of Frederick and his wife, Miriam Sargent. Maud's possible father in this theory was therefore known to the family, or at least to Walter.

However, Maud's medical notes from when she was an in-patient at the Lady Chichester Hospital in 1922 reveal something quite different about the identity of her father. The doctor's consultation notes reveal that she was the illegitimate daughter of a mentally deficient sister and a brother (*The Keep*, Medical Report, 1922, 3–4). This provides insight as to why the father was a source of shame within the Eades family; if there had indeed been a physical union between a brother and sister which resulted in the birth of Maud. The medical notes also show that Maud claimed she was not illegitimate and that it was a story made up by relatives (*The Keep*, East Sussex Records, Medical Report, 1922, 9). Perhaps she was referring to the point that the family did know the identity of the father, rather than just being illegitimate.

If Maud was being truthful to her doctor, it gives greater weight to the theory that it was an uncle of hers who was her father and may explain why both Emma and Maud were virtually shunned by the family. Whoever the father was, be it an uncle or a friend of the family, it is understandable perhaps why, at that time, the father was un-named on Maud's birth certificate, particularly in such moralistic times.

For continuity purposes, Maud will now be referred to as Gill, Mrs Gill or Madge Gill; the latter being the name she was known by as an artist and medium.

Interbreeding and illegitimacy were again to touch Gill's life. The former theme was borne out through her marriage to her first cousin, Thomas Edwin Gill; and the latter by their first son, Lawrence ('Laurie') Edwin Gill, who was born in September of 1906, outside of marriage. The couple eventually married on 1st January, 1907 (www.madgegill.com), and it is noteworthy that there were inaccuracies recorded on their marriage certificate. For example, Gill is recorded as being 'Madge Ethel Eades' (the middle name being a new addition) and she also puts her age as 25 when, in fact, she was still 24. Her father's name is recorded as 'William Frederick Eades' and it has been suggested that this was probably a fabricated name (ibid). The situation of their first son being born illegitimately must have touched Gill, perhaps bringing back feelings of how she was ostracised by some members of her family (as well as society) for being born out of wedlock.

Becoming pregnant by her first cousin, Thomas Gill may well have contributed to the many gynaecological complications that she experienced. In the early 1900s, it was not uncommon to marry one's cousin. However, since then, medical research has proved that a 'cousin marriage' – therefore being a close blood relative – is a known risk factor for complications in birth and pregnancy (SANDS, communication to Author). Gill did indeed experience some difficulties, which were borne out by her miscarriages in between pregnancies, as well as giving birth to a stillborn daughter – all of which understandably devastated her.

Returning now to Gill's wider family; her mother, Emma Elizabeth Eades, was the second daughter of William Baxter Eades and his wife Caroline (née Wright). Emma's siblings were; William Issac, Harry, Walter, Alfred and Kate, Caroline (also known as Carrie) and Alice (www.madgegill.com). Her brother Walter lived with her (Emma) at home in Primrose Road, Woodford, and he was the informant of her death on the 11th December, 1913 (GRO, Eades' death certificate). Her certificate recorded that she died of 'fatty degeneration of the heart and cerebral haemorrhage.' Sadly, Walter died very shortly after Emma (www.freebmd), aged approximately 57. He left no wife or children of his own and it appears that he was Emma's guardian long after their parents had both died (their father in 1881 and their mother in 1897). By the time Walter had reached his midfifties he was apparently "a lonely man and given to outbursts of temper" (www.madgegill.com). Possibly, he was living with depression and may have been exhausted and overwhelmed by the tiring responsibility of being Emma's carer and dependant.

Prior to Gill's birth, her family lived at 2a Charlotte Street (now Hallam Street, W1.), off Portland Place in Marylebone. This was the office for of the United and Central Synagogue (Dutton, 2019, 107). The Eades family shared their home with Jacob Cohen, the assistant beadle for the synagogue. William Eades was employed as a caretaker at the synagogue (www.ancestry.co.uk – 1871 Census) and his duties were important. Jewish people are not permitted to work on Saturdays or Jewish holidays (Yom Tov) and at these times synagogues can be at their busiest. Therefore, it is essential that synagogue caretakers are not Jewish, for very practical reasons (personal correspondence to the Author from Mick Frankel).

The aforementioned address in Walthamstow, where Gill was born, was home to an elderly couple called Joseph and Sarah Leakey who were 82 and 79, respectively. The 1891 Census shows that Mr and Mrs Leakey had their two adult daughters (both in their forties) living with them; Emma (who was a school mistress) and Mary Ann. In addition to the two daughters living there was also an adopted seven year old daughter, Edith Leakey. Gill was listed as being a boarder, as well as a young boy called Bertram Browning. It is highly probable that the young children were home educated there by Emma Leakey, the school mistress.

Being an unmarried mother in the Victorian era was considered reprehensible and scandalous, due to society's moral principles. Thankfully, attitudes have progressed significantly since then. It is unknown how the Eades family knew the Leakey family but Emma's parents sent her to live with them until after her baby was born. The Eades family allowed Emma to return to the family home in Charlotte Street and Gill was left in the care of Mr and Mrs Leakey.

The Eades family doctor held the opinion that Emma Eades would have been unable to raise her child (www.madgegill.com); this may have been because she had learning difficulties and/or mental health issues. It has been said that Emma was "reported to have been of feeble character and unable to bring up a child" (ibid). Feeble-mindedness was a term associated at that time with people with mental, physical and sensory disabilities (www.historicengland.org.uk).

Seemingly, Mr and Mrs Eades were embarrassed about their daughter having an illegitimate child but were supportive in that Emma was permitted to return home, albeit without her baby. In her lifetime, Emma had always lived with a member of her family and Census records show that she was never in employment. This shows that she was dependent on her family providing for her. In those times, people living with disabilities and/or learning difficulties were often hidden away at home and not permitted to work (ibid). As previously discussed, her brother Walter cared for Emma through much of her adult years.

There is the possibility that her father's employers would have frowned upon an unmarried mother being associated with their Synagogue and that was part of the reason why Emma had to go away until her child was born and forced to give up her child. The whole experience must have been bewildering and traumatic for Emma. Her father, William Baxter Eades, made weekly financial contributions to the Leakey's towards caring for Gill. After a while, Gill's grandfather could no longer maintain the financial agreement for reasons pertaining to his ill-health and unemployment, so for a short while Maud was looked after by her Aunt Kate. Interestingly, after Madge Gill died, her eldest son Lawrence wrote to Louise Morgan – a friend of his mother's. She was interested in learning more about Madge's childhood.

He told her that his mother was brought up as a child by a governess, a Mrs Nunn of Danbury, Essex, who was sister-in-law to a 'Nunn' Q.C. (Dutton, 2019, 172). However, the Author's research shows that whilst Thomas Hancock Nunn was admitted to the Inner Temple law courts on the 26th April, 1881, he was never appointed as Queen's Counsel (https://archives.innertemple.org.uk).

Clearly, there was some confusion or misunderstanding about Thomas Hancock Nunn and his position. Perhaps it was a story fabricated by Gill that she told her son, especially if she was embarrassed about her early life, or perhaps she had no recall about that period of her life. It is of course possible that Lawrence concocted the story to help fill a void about his mother's life that he had little or no knowledge of.

Thomas Hancock Nunn's story is interesting, however, for he went on to become a social reformer and through his vast work formed the foundations of what went on to become the London Council of Social Service (https://en.wikipedia.org/wiki). The aforementioned governess, Mrs Nunn, was wife of John Hancock Nunn (brother of Thomas) and he was involved with the Indian Rubber business, which was founded by his brother (ibid).

Returning now to Gill's care when she was a child. As previously noted, for a short period Gill's Aunt Kate temporarily cared for her. However, in 1891, a decision was made by the family to transfer her into the Village Homes of Dr. Barnardo's (www.madgegill.com) which was in Barkingside, Essex. This institute was known for caring for destitute children. Kate informed them that the family were unable to financially support Gill at the Leakey's anymore. Supporting the application, the Eades' family doctor, Edward James Nix of Great Portland Street (www.ancestry.co.uk – 1891 Census), testified that Emma was unfit to look after her daughter (Dutton, 2019, 236). The Eades family signed the 'Canada Clause' when they handed Gill into Barnardo's care and this gave authorisation for her to be shipped abroad for work purposes (Dutton, 2019, 237/Ayad).

When she moved to Barnardo's, initially Gill spent a fortnight at the Barnardo's Receiving Home where she would have been medically assessed and eased into her new environment. Then she would have been moved into a cottage with around fifteen other girls who were cared for by a 'cottage mother' who was an "earnest-minded Christian lady" (Dutton, 2019, 236/Ayad).

MADGE GILL 1882–1961

Barnardo's Village Home for Girls, Essex with church on right c.1901 by permission of Redbridge Museum & Heritage Centre.

Her role was to train the young children for useful and industrial lives. At the Village Home Gill would have been taught reading, writing and arithmetic, as well as domestic work, needlework and nursing. Christian singing was also encouraged and Bible classes and twice-daily prayers were obligatory (Dutton, 2019, 237/Ayad). Barnardo's favoured hymn book was *Sankey's Hymn Book* – a standard issue for the children (*Raw Vision*, Ayad, 30). Ira D. Sankey was an American composer and gospel singer.

In 1896, Gill along with thousands of other British children weas shipped out to Canada as part of the 'Home Children's Scheme'. This was a labour programme which was supposed to offer opportunities and prospects to underprivileged children. The scheme was Britain's attempt at helping to combat poverty. Orphans and children who lived in poverty were sent to Australia and Canada to live with families and improve their lives. The children were expected to work in exchange for room and board.

Maud Eades c. 1896 licensed by Barnardo's Picture Library.

Gill travelled with 255 other children as steerage passengers on the steamship 'Scotsman' on 30th July, 1896. They arrived at their destination in Quebec on 8th August, 1896. Maud Eades was listed as a twelve year old servant on the ship's passenger list. Just one man, a 'Mr Owen', was responsible for the huge numbers of children. Along with the other young girls, Maud was taken to Hazelbrae House in Peterbrough, Ontario which was known as 'The Girls Distributing Centre' (www.recherche-collection).

Being a steerage passenger must have been a harrowing experience for the children and not the great adventure crossing seas they probably anticipated. The term 'steerage' originated in the fact that passengers could only sleep in the machinery area of the ship and not in cabins. The conditions were normally dark and damp with limited sanitation and stormy seas could make it dirty and foul-smelling. Diseases such as typhus and dysentery were rife, as were rat and insect infestation (www.history.com).

The former home of Mr and Mrs Rae in Peterborough, Ontario where Maud Eades was indentured as a servant. Photo with kind permission from Lori Oschefski of 'Home Children Canada'.

Steerage was also a euphemism for extreme poverty, hardship and suffering. For those passengers, it was an experience fraught with danger and disease. Some surviving children who sailed to Canada vividly remember the smell of sea sickness, as many children were terribly ill on board and they were permitted on the deck of the ship for exercise and fresh air only. The children slept at the bottom of the ship in cramped quarters with no windows (L. Oschefski, BHCARA, communication to Author).

Gill's time in Canada was spent as a domestic servant and child-minder (http://www.madgegill.com); she was twelve years old at this time. She worked hard and was especially fond of the first family who employed her – Mr and Mrs Rae. She remained in employment with them for three years. It seems that she was treated with kindness and respect, was supported by them and was provided with access to education whilst she lived with them. Gill was also able to develop her creativity through crocheting, embroidery and sewing (Camic, 2013, 3) whilst living with them. However, she was still anxious to return home and left the Rae's employment for higher wages from other employers. Her plan was to save sufficient money in order to sail back to England. Subsequently, she went on to work for three other families who were less than kind and not supportive to her. Gill did not remain in their employment for very long (ibid). The amount which employers paid to a child or young person depended on various factors including their age, the type of job they were doing, how often they were attending school and the area they were located in within Canada. The amount paid would have been negotiated between Barnardo's and the employer on an individual basis, depending on what the boarding agreement was. The amount paid to the child would have increased as they got older and it was re-negotiated on an annual basis (Archives Manager at Barnardo's Making Connections).

By November of 1900, Gill was back in England from Canada, having sailed again as a steerage passenger on the 'Corinthus' which landed in Liverpool with hundreds of other children on board (https://www.britishhomechildren.com – The National Archives, Form 20, Passenger Lists). She must have been exhausted and weary. In September of 2021, a memorial was unveiled for the thousands of children brought from England to the Hazelbrae Home in Canada. Her given name 'Maud Eades' is one of the many names inscribed on the memorial stone (www.canadianbritishhomechildren.weebly.com -Lori Oschefski).

Gill was almost nineteen years old when she went to live with one of the Leakey daughters (Mary Ann Leaky) who by then was a Head Mistress and still living in Walthamstow (http://www.madgegill.com). By now, Gill was calling herself 'Madge'. She quickly gained employment as a blouse machinist and then later found work as a probationary nurse (ibid) at the nearby West Ham Union Workhouse in Leytonstone, which became the West Ham Infirmary. Then, in 1917, it became known as (and remains) Whipps Cross Hospital (www.bartshealth.nhs.uk). Duties required to be undertaken by nurses at infirmaries included: to work a twelve-hour day, to read prayers to the patients every night before 7.30pm (all patients previously having been put to bed), Nurses then had to ensure that all fires were made-up, scuttles filled and gas lowered before going off duty (www.health.hackneysociety.org). Then, as today, the working life of a nurse was extremely hard.

Three years later, Gill was in a relationship with her cousin Thomas Edwin Gill, he apparently "felt sorry for the way life had treated her" (Cardinal, 1972, 135). In 1906, they had their first son, Lawrence ('Laurie') Edwin Gill. He was born out of wedlock, as previously noted, but the Gill's married in January of the following year (http://www.madgegill.com). Then, in 1910, they had their second son, Reginald Alfred Gill (ibid). A third son, Leonard Eric ('Bob') Gill, was born three years later. Tragically, their young son, Reggie, died in 1918, as a result of the Spanish Flu epidemic. By this time, Thomas was deeply concerned about his wife's mental health which had significantly deteriorated since the death of their second son.

In 1919, Thomas Gill returned from serving in the First World War and, like so many, he struggled to find employment – money was scarce and the family were poor. However, it would seem the

Front cover for the sheet music of 'Home Sweet Home'. Public domain via Wikipedia: Project Gutenberg. e-text 21566.

family were not always financially challenged. Before the First World War, they were seemingly comfortable and financially secure, at least for a while. The *Woodford Rate Book* for April 1913 shows Thomas Gill was living at Fern Cottage, George Lane in Woodford. He rented a house with a garden for his family at the sum of 25 pounds a year, with rates of 1/5 a month. This was a colossal amount of money in 1913. In order to afford such high rent for a property in an affluent area like Woodford, Thomas Gill must have been employed and had sufficient financial security at that particular time in his life (Redbridge Museum & Heritage Centre).

In March 1920, Gill started to receive great creative inspiration (www.madgegill.com) and what started as an ordinary day later turned into an extraordinary day for her. She was attending to her household chores as normal but unusually started to sing at the top of her voice *'Home Sweet Home'*. This was a popular and successful ballad published in 1914 and was later recorded by popular singers, Bing Crosby and Vera Lynn. A line from the song is exceptionally apt given what happened to Gill on that remarkable day: "A charm from the sky seems to hallow us there."

The words are significant because whilst Gill was singing that song, she also felt compelled to go into her garden, which she did, taking her two sons with her. All three of them looked up at the sky (*The Keep*, East Sussex Records, Med. Records, 6); they saw the clouds part and saw a vision of Christ on a cross in the sky surrounded by angels (ibid). The song that she felt inspired to sing (*Home Sweet Home*) is interesting – could it be that 'home' meant a 'spiritual haven' for Gill? The epiphany was surely confirmation to her that there was a higher force at work in the material world, thus enforcing her belief and faith in a spiritual life. This was something she was made aware of by her religious upbringing through her Barnardo's education.

The aforementioned vision which the three family members saw in the garden must have been astonishing and mystifying for her young sons. Perhaps it opened up a new way of seeing and understanding the world. Possibly, it helped them formulate their own philosophy and meaning of life. One example of this can be seen whereby Lawrence, like his mother and Uncle Bert, became a member of The Theosophical Society. He was approximately

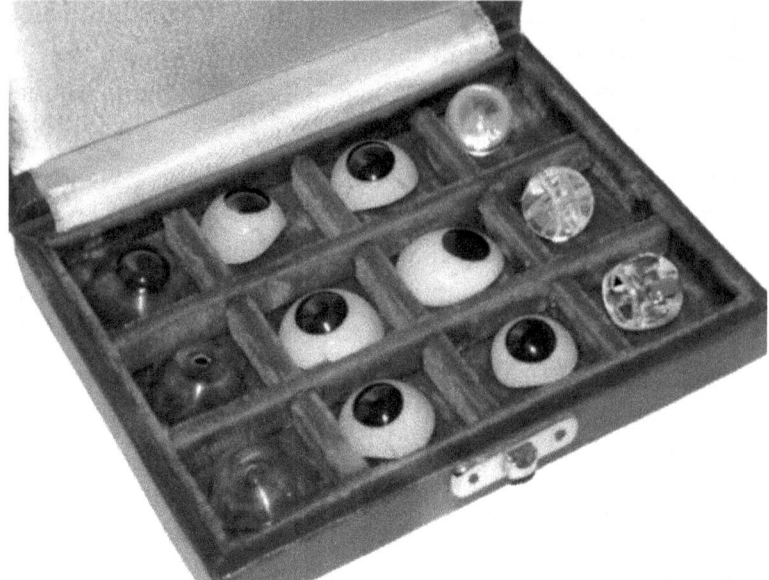

Glass eyes boxed c.1920: from museum curator at the College of Optometrists.

eighteen years old when he joined the organisation (www.madgegill.com) but at the time of the apparition was just thirteen years old.

After the epiphany, Gill started to "draw, sing, knit, sew and write automatically" (www.madgegill.com) and in her lifetime it is estimated that she produced thousands of pieces of work – more detail about her arts and talents will be discussed further on.

The year 1920 was a significant one for her as she was also diagnosed with cancer and as a result had to have her left eye removed and it was replaced with a glass one. The impact this had on Maud entailed her having to adapt to monocular vision, which may have altered her perception of depth and she may have found it harder to judge distances. Lack of peripheral vision may have meant that she had to learn to turn her head to a greater extent and, although she may have adapted well in a short space of time, there may have been an increase in the risk of her falling (www.college-optometrists.org). Certainly, in the penultimate year of her life, she had falls which placed her in hospital (Dutton, 2019, 171). Gill had experienced several health problems (The Keep, East Sussex Records, Medical Report) throughout her lifetime. At nine years old, she had diphtheria and an ulcerated leg and, when she was approximately 36, she had all of her teeth removed as her gums were all sceptic. In addition to all of this, she had a hernia and, as discussed earlier, she had her left eye removed following a diagnosis of cancer (www.madgegill.com). When she arrived at the Lady Chichester Hospital, she was undernourished as she had not been eating properly (The Keep, Medical Records, Letter).

The experience of Gill giving birth to a stillborn daughter in 1921 must have been truly devastating for her, especially as she was desperate to have a daughter, plus she had already experienced the death of her son, Reginald, as well as miscarriages in between the births of all of her sons. Care in the 1920s was very different for women to what it is today. Women who had experienced pregnancy loss or the death of a baby would not normally have been able to see their baby. The health professionals would have taken the baby away and made arrangements without involving or informing the parent (SANDS, communication to Author).

Unsurprisingly, Gill's mental health had deteriorated even further. It is possible that she was living with what we now know but didn't know then to be post-traumatic stress disorder (PTSD). Not only did she experience the aforementioned losses, but there were also the deaths of the older members of her family.

There were also many lives lost during the First World War, which included 162 civilians (of which eighteen were children from an infant's school) in Poplar, East London. The attack by the Germans was as a result of the first daylight air raids on the 13th June, 1917. Zeppelins dropped over 100 bombs and East London was hit very badly by the bombing. Naturally, many people were traumatised by this horrific event. Aside from being virtually surrounded by death, other contributing factors to Gill's ill-heath may have been financial insecurity, as well as her husband's infidelity, which will be discussed further on.

In 1921, her husband instigated her getting proper rest and treatment. Before he approached the charity the Essex Voluntary Association, they had spoken to a doctor who suggested that Gill should have psycho-analytical treatment at the Bethlem Asylum. When Thomas Gill wrote to the voluntary organisation, he explained to the secretary, Miss C.A. Nevile, what the previous doctor had advised. He added that Gill was set against going to a lunatic asylum, as through her work as an infirmary nurse she knew what that would entail (The Keep, East Sussex Records, Letter dated 01/09/2021). Mr Gill agreed with his wife and put to C.A. Neville that his wife never harmed anyone and that it was inappropriate for her to go to such a hospital. Clearly, he still cared for his wife, irrespective of his adultery.

The Bethlem Hospital still exists today and is the oldest psychiatric hospital since 1247 (www.nhs.uk). When Miss Nevile first approached Dr Boyle (who ran the Lady Chichester Hospital) about Gill, she wrote: "My own feeling is that she ought to go to a place like Bethlem or failing that is really bad enough for certification" (The Keep, East Sussex Records, Letter dated 01/09/1922, page 2). Ironically, since then, 'Madge Gill' has been the subject of a blog written for Bethlem's Museum of the Mind website (www.museumofthemind.org.uk).

Fortunately, Gill was accepted as an inpatient in January 1922, at the progressive hospital for children and women in Hove. The Lady Chichester Hospital specialised in treating the patients for early nervous disorders. It was run by Dr Helen Alice Anne Boyle. Gill's skills and talents were actively encouraged by Dr Boyle. While she was in hospital, Gill gave character readings to the other inpatients and also spoke in 'other tongues' when asked. Some of her medical notes show that the unknown languages may have been 'Basque', as spoken in villages in between

Lady Chichester Hospital, Hove – postcard. Photographer unknown.

France and Spain, although at first it wasn't certain (The Keep, Medical Record, page 2). Dr Boyle eventually summarised that she thought the languages to be Arabic, Basque and Hindustani (Dutton, 2019, 109/Ayad). Boyle had a special interest in her patient (and possibly in spiritualism) and in March of 1922 she approached the Society for Psychical Research in London for their views about the languages that Gill was able to speak. The organisation's research officer, Eric Dingwall, refused to have Gill's speech recorded. He claimed that Gill's language "appeared to be a very ordinary made-up language and presents nothing very extraordinary" (ibid). Boyle was determined to have the speech recorded and just a few days before Gill was discharged from the hospital, her unknown languages were recorded on a dictaphone by her colleague Mr Rhonda Williams (The Keep, Medical Record, page 3).

On 18th April, 1922, she was discharged from the hospital. Then, along with her husband and two sons, she went to live with family members Kate and Bert Gill. There she found a conducive and sympathetic environment for her creativity and

Dr. Helen Boyle c.1909. Public domain – Wikipedia.

spiritual interests, which included automatic writing (http://www.madgegill.com). It was a favourable setting for Gill as it is believed that Kate was also a spiritualist and could 'tell-fortunes'. In addition, Kate's husband, Bert, established The British College of Astrology, advertising it in *The Occult Review* publication. He stated that he was the secretary (ibid). Then, in 1919, he joined a local branch of the Theosophical Society in Bow (ibid). Clearly, this branch of the family was familiar with esoteric subjects (ibid).

Gill's doctor, Dr Boyle, is herself worthy of digression from Gill's biography. The aforementioned hospital in Hove was founded by Dr Alice Helen Anne Boyle and her practice partner, Dr Mabel Jones, in 1905. It had originally started as a progressive clinic "for early nervous and borderland cases among women and children" (Dutton, 2019, 107/Ayad). Gill was 38 when she was admitted to the hospital, which by then was called the Lady Chichester Hospital for the Treatment of Early Mental Disorders. Boyle observed through her past working experience in the East End (e.g.Claybury Hospital and Canning Town Mission Hospital) that women who had neither a certifiable physical disease nor certifiable mental illness, were often caught between an asylum and an infirmary (ibid) and she called this situation 'borderland'. The term meant women who were between the beginnings of a mental breakdown and incurable insanity. Boyle saw the mental and physical strain put upon working class women living in poverty.

She believed that a timely and sympathetic intervention at the start of a mental breakdown could prevent the patient from slipping into incurable insanity (ibid). At that time, disorders such as anxiety, depression and obsessive-compulsive disorder were not considered serious enough to treat. However, Dr Boyle thought differently. One of the principles of the Lady Chichester Hospital was provision of treatment for women by women and it was the first hospital of its kind (https://www.npg.org.uk).

Boyle's holistic therapies were tailored to an individual's need. Treatments included a nourishing diet, gentle exercise for mind and body, as well as rest and also recreational activities such as attending concerts and theatre productions. Patients were also expected to undertake light domestic duties. Dr Boyle actively encouraged Gill's art and just one year after Gill was discharged from the hospital, she participated in her first art exhibition (ibid).

After she was discharged from the hospital, Gill wrote to Dr Boyle informing her of her achievement. Clearly, Dr Boyle had a positive impact on Gill and she understood her need to create and make. Interestingly, both Dr Boyle and Madge Gill were recognised for their achievements and, posthumously, each was awarded a Blue Heritage Plaque; Gill in 2019 and Boyle in 2015. The latter was a pioneer in her time. For example; she was Brighton's first female general practitioner; she was the first female president of the Royal Medico-Psychological Association in 1939, now known as The Royal College of Psychiatrists. She was also involved with The National Association for Mental Health, which today is known as the charity Mind (https://www.mind.org.uk/about-us/our-achievements). Interestingly, author and occultist, Dion Fortune, was a patient and then later a lay-analyst at the Medico-Psychological Clinic in 1914 (Miles, 2022, 107).

Returning to Gill's life now. From the end of 1922, she was in the spotlight, including the national newspaper *The Sunday Express* and the spiritualist newspaper, *LIGHT* – the publications carried features about her artwork and mediumship. This was the start of her coming into the spotlight and attracting other artists and spiritualists to her work, Sir Arthur Conan Doyle being one such person (http://www.madegill.com). Between 1932 and 1947, she exhibited her art for the East End Academy at the Whitechapel Gallery, and extensive archives at the gallery show that she attracted press coverage and, on several occasions, even headlines (www.academia.edu). In November 1939, *The Times* newspaper described Madge Gill as having a curious talent (ibid).

In 1942, Gill was featured in the spiritualist newspaper, *Psychic News*. The feature was about Gill's creations being displayed at the *Artists Aid Russia Exhibition,* the editorial was entitled: 'Unseen' Forces Guide Artist (*Psychic News*, 1942, 3). Earlier, in 1923, she was one of the various artists selected by author and spiritualist, William Tylar, to show her work at an exhibition that he was co-ordinating at the International Congress of Spiritualists in Belgium.

Clearly, it was a changing time in her life, where she felt confident enough to showcase her work. In August of 1942 (and as previously noted), Gill participated in the *Artists Aid Russia Exhibition* where she, along with celebrated artists such as Duncan Grant and L.S. Lowry, showcased their work. The exhibition was held at The Wallace Collection in Hertford House in Marylebone, London (Dutton, 2019, 142). It was co-ordinated by Winston Churchill's wife, Clementine Churchill, as a fundraising exercise; she was Chairman of the Red Cross Aid to the Russian Fund.

In 1930–31, Gill's son, Leonard, aged seventeen, was involved in a motorcycle accident and as a result he suffered with a broken neck. For several years Gill nursed him constantly, remaining at his bedside for hours, sometimes drawing in semi-darkness for hours (www.madgegill.com). This may have also been for practical reasons. It is well known in spiritualist circles that it is conducive to work in semi-darkness, if possible, as this condition helps to develop the power needed for certain tasks such as automatic writing (Carrington, 1975, 147). Eventually, Leonard did recover but he was left with disabilities.

Later, in 1932, she exhibited her work for the first time at the Whitechapel Gallery in East London (this was for the East End Academy) she continued to exhibit her artwork there until 1947. During 1933, Gill became a widow; her husband, aged 50, died of carcinoma (cancer) of the lungs in Whipps Cross Hospital. Lawrence E. Gill was the informant of his father's death (GRO, death certificate for Thomas Gill).

In 1937, the occult magazine, *Prediction*, published an extensive interview with Gill. She was photographed by Peter West and named as 'Mrs Madge E. Gill' and the article was entitled: 'The Problem of Inspired Art' (LIGHT, 2019, 47). In 1938, she started to advertise herself as an astrologer in local newspapers, such as *The Chelmsford* Chronicle, calling herself 'Kharmastra' and she charged a moderate fee for her services (www.madegegill.com). This is interesting as she adamantly refused to sell her artwork in her lifetime. It seems that she was confident in her knowledge of astrology and in providing a service for the general public. She also generated astrology charts for her friends and used black and red ink to create the natal charts (Cardinal, 1972, 137).

Gill extended her spiritualist activities by the mid-1930s, whereby she held weekly séances in her house which involved table-turnings and using the Ouija board (ibid). Celebrated author and spiritual healer, Harry Edwards, wrote in his book about developing mediumship that for students wishing to do so, they should avoid using the method of the Ouja board. His advice and guidance being that so-called 'communications' obtained in this way were 'unreliable' as well as 'elemental and crude'. By the mid-1930s, Gill was in her early-fifties and one would hope that, if she was regularly using this practice by then, she had the experience and wisdom of how to use the Ouija board responsibly and safely. It seems that Edwards was not a fan of 'table communications' as he advised his readers: "Have nothing to do with it – at any time" (Edwards, 2003, 36).

In 1940, Gill along with her sons and brother-in-law, Bert, moved to 37 Plashet Grove in Upton Park; Bert's wife had died in 1929. Previously, Gill had lived at 7 Thorngrove Road in Upton Park, having moved there in 1918 from South Woodford. Sadly, Bert died in 1948 and then, in 1950, Gill's son Leonard died (www.madgegill.com). Her last piece of work is thought to have been created in 1958 (ibid.). Three years later, she died in Langthorne

Hospital in Leytonstone. The hospital existed primarily for long-stay 'geriatric' patients and it was probably in this capacity that Madge was admitted (www.bartshealthnhstrust.co.uk).

Her last son, Lawrence Gill, died two years after his mother. However, always supportive of her work and capabilities, he made a strategic decision before he died. He donated vast amounts of her work to East Ham Council, which was cared for then by the borough librarian, James Green. Today it is the Newham Archives and Local Studies Library that holds much of Madge Gill's work, especially the postcard art. However, much of her art is now in private collections in the United Kingdom and around the world.

ASTROLOGY IN ACTION

The following quote is by Myrinerest – Gill's spirit guide (*LIGHT*, 2019, 23):

> "Stars are the luminous orbs which guide the weary traveller and map the destiny of each one existing upon the material plane. The stars are the spiritual bodies of activity."

WHAT MADGE GILL'S RECTIFIED NATAL CHART SHOWS

Madge Gill became famous as an artist and medium, coming into the spotlight in approximately 1922 and again in the 1930s and 1940s by exhibiting her artwork. Posthumously, she became known as an 'Outsider Artist' – the expression was coined by Roger Cardinal, a free-thinking art historian and scholar. He was best known for his 1972 book, *Outsider Art*, in which Gill was included. The term is used to describe art that has a naive quality and is usually produced by people who are not trained or haven't worked as artists within the conventional structures

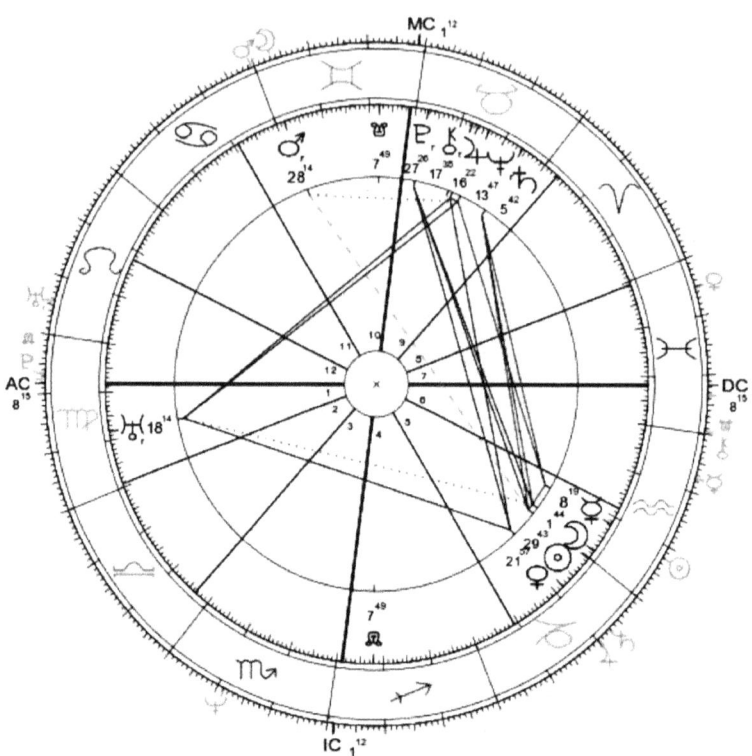

Madge Gill's rectified natal chart and the transits to it on the day she died, 28th January, 1961

of art production (www.tate.org.uk/art/art-terms). Gill told a journalist in 1922: "I am no artist, in the ordinary sense of the word" (*LIGHT*, June 2019, 25), showing an awareness of her unorthodox style of art. In a letter to her friend, Louise Morgan, Gill confides in her: "I wish I could be normal" (Cardinal, 1972, 138).

As we know, Gill was born on the 19th January, 1882 (www.madegill.com), in Walthamstow but we do not know her time of birth, which is crucial to generate a precise birth chart. However, by using a process called rectification (*see glossary*); a birth time can often be concluded. This process involves looking at significant events in Gill's life and the transiting outer planets at her natal chart at the time of the occasion. Then, by interpreting the aspects (*see glossary*), this helps to conclude a time of birth (or as near as possible a time). Having undertaken this process, the time of Gill's birth was calculated as 20.00pm GMT.

Her rectified natal chart comprises of the following astrological information: two stelliums (*see glossary*) – one in the fifth house the other in the ninth house, an earth Grand Trine (*see glossary*) and a preponderance of the fixed mode (*see glossary*), a prevalence of the earth element and, finally, on the axis all four angles (*see glossary*) which belong to the mutable mode (*see glossary*). But what does this all mean?

The stelliums show a close cluster of three or more planets in one (or more) house (*see glossary*). In Gill's natal chart, as previously noted, it is in the fifth house and ninth house. The former house is associated with children, love affairs and creativity whilst the latter governs belief, church, faith, long distance travel, freedom, higher education, religion and its mythology, politics, morals and publishing. These two houses indicate areas of her life where there would be tremendous activity and energy. The earth Grand Trine shows that Gill was enormously practical and self-sufficient. One obvious example of this is her exemplary skill in embroidery and dress-making, it also shows that she worked hard and was resourceful.

The preponderance of planets in the fixed signs shows that Gill could be determined and indomitable, to the point of stubbornness at times. However, the mutable mode on the axis in her natal chart could help to lessen and soften the resolute side of her nature when necessary. This indicates that in her life Gill was able to adapt and adjust, could be flexible but could also be prone to being agitated, restless and perhaps overly nervous. The ASC is Virgo, the IC is Sagittarius, the DSC is Pisces and the MC is Gemini and they will be discussed in more detail further on (*see glossary for definitions of all the axis positions*).

CAPRICORN, SATURN AND RELATIONSHIPS

The Sun was in Capricorn at 29 degrees when Gill was born and when a sign is at that point it is described as a 'critical degree'. This is because it is thought to add an extra challenge when it is placed there at the time of one's birth (or when a transiting planet arrives at that point) – the difficulty being that it is about to leave one sign and enter another.

Capricorn is an earth sign; action orientated and is ruled by Saturn. By nature, Capricorn is practical, realistic, conscientious and disciplined with a strong work ethic. It is considered the conservative sign of the zodiac as it upholds authority and tradition and seeks to be efficient and organised. Capricorns are generally cautious and reserved, as well as conservative and serious about their work. As they are comfortable with control and regulations; some Capricorns may be drawn to esoteric subjects since it involves working with cosmic laws. Certainly, Gill upheld the Eades family tradition in that all the women (apart from two) remained in the family home and were never in employment.

The professional name 'Kharmastra' that Gill used to advertise her astrological services is noteworthy. It is a combination of 'Karma' and 'Astra' meaning star. The 'Kh' at the beginning of the name suggests the "ch" sound as in the Hebrew word "chaim" which means life (Mick Frankel in communication to Author). Karma is pertinent to Saturn – the ruler of Gill's Sun sign, Capricorn. This is because Saturn is often termed 'Lord Karma' (because it is associated with the lessons of life) and, because it is disciplined, it can both award and punish. At times, Capricorns can be seen as 'long-suffering' people who experience plenty of burdens and obstacles, but equally they can be seen as a controlled and motivated sign. Saturn allows for quiet ambition and personal growth but only through one's fulfilment of duties and responsibilities, it does not allow for short-cuts and superficiality. Capricorns often find achievement and success for their ambitions later in life, and this was certainly true in Gill's life but more so after her death.

Saturn is also known as Old Father Time – the figure with his scythe held in his bony hand which is ready to remove from our lives all that is unnecessary. He is the figure of death, the Grim Reaper. Obstacles, restrictions and trials may be part of the personal growth, as these are lessons that Saturn brings to test upon us. If acceptance and patience as well as accountability and necessity can be applied then strength and wisdom can be gained. Saturn therefore acts as reaper as well as teacher; the latter because, through our stumbling blocks and tribulations, one can gain maturity and wisdom.

It is interesting that Saturn has also been described not only as the Grim Reaper but also as the 'priest-initiate' (Hodgson, 2005, 104), which is pertinent to Gill and her spirit guide. She told a newspaper reporter in 1922: "The spirit who comes to me is that of a high priest. He lived in ancient Babylon" (*LIGHT*, 2019, 25), which shows the Saturn connection of authority and wisdom.

Venus is also positioned in Capricorn in Gill's natal chart and suggests that she was serious about her relationships. Certainly, in relations of the heart she would have been under no illusions about love; conceiving it perhaps as 'the business of love.' She may have entered into relationships for the security and status she believed it could bring her and been of the belief that 'marriage was for life.'

There seems to be nothing known about her partnerships other than that of her husband, Thomas Gill. Mercury is in the fifth house of her natal chart and suggests that she needed a partner who was as intelligent as she was. Thomas may have been as bright as his wife but it is believed he did not share the same esoteric interests as she did. Her descendant (*see glossary*) is in Pisces which indicates that Mrs Gill was also looking for compassion, kindness and sensitivity in her partnerships, since these are some of the qualities associated with Pisces.

Thomas Edwin Gill was an Aries Sun and Moon sign (http://www.astro.com), he was born on 21st March, 1882 (https://madgegill.com/chronology). He is described in his military records as being 5' 8" with a 37" chest, brown hair, grey eyes and an olive complexion (ibid). He enlisted to fight in the First World War in 1917 and was selected for the navy role; he served on three ships which included The Aberdeen. His character and ability are described on his service record as being very good and satisfactory (National Archives, ADM).

Some of the qualities associated with Aries include assertion and courage, as well as being bombastic and impulsive. If this is true of Thomas, it may have caused some problems within their marriage, by him being perhaps hot-headed and impatient with his wife. This is because Aries is known as 'the baby of the zodiac.' It is the first sign in the astrology calendar and has much to learn about compromise and patience with other signs. Aries is a fire sign, so Thomas may have brought some much-needed spontaneity and warmth to their relationship, an energy which is lacking in his wife's natal chart.

Their marriage ran into problems. Exactly when things started to deteriorate is unknown but it included Thomas Gill having extramarital affairs. Possibly, his wife knew about them and gave him her blessing to carry on with the affairs. Perhaps she just didn't care. She may well have wanted to conserve the status quo of the marriage and not enter into a separation, which would not have been easy for a woman then, either economically or legally. For example, it was not until 1923 under the Matrimonial Causes Act that a woman could divorce her husband on the grounds of adultery. Madge would have been approximately 41 in that year. It was considered scandalous by society at that time for women to be divorced, especially working-class women.

It is possible Gill may have wanted to continue her relationship with Thomas for security purposes and may have taken a pragmatic attitude towards her husband's philandering. She may also have felt an aloofness and detachment towards the situation. This is because in her natal chart the Moon is in Aquarius. This position suggests dispassionate and logical emotions and it is also associated with erratic emotions, such are some of the qualities associated with Aquarius. Being concerned with honesty is another attribute of this sign. This position suggests that Gill may have wanted the stark truth about the situation and not wanted her intelligence insulted regarding his affairs. The aspect Venus trine Pluto also shows that she could deal with any crisis and intensity in a relationship. This is because Venus is associated with partnerships, whilst Pluto is associated with pain and trauma. Irrespective of their relationship breakdown, Thomas evidently did still care about his wife and her ill-health, for he initiated getting the best care possible for her when her mental health was significantly deteriorating.

APPEARANCE AND IMPRESSION

Gill's ascendant Virgo suggests that she liked to present herself in a neat and tidy demeanour (something crucial for her role as a nurse) and that she liked to feel smart but not overdressed. She has been described as "a small, slim person, very neat in appearance, but painfully shy of strangers" (Dutton, 2019, 202).

Publicity shots of her were taken at her home in Plashet Grove in 1947, by the society photographer, Edward Russell Westwood. At this point, she may have been feeling more confident about her abilities and talents. His photographs and interview were supposed to have appeared in *The Illustrated News* publication when Gill was 65. Sadly, the feature was never run, which may have made Gill feel rejected, frustrated or not good enough. In the photographs, she wore both a vividly coloured print dress that she made herself using different threads, as well as a block plain dress made from balloon material. One photograph illustrated her hands at work and the editorial accompanying the image perfectly describes Gill's resourceful and unique abilities: "... busy at work on an original piece of embroidery made from old scraps of coloured wool" (www.gettyimages.co.uk).

The Virgo ascendant may also have created the impression to people that she was a perfectionist with exacting standards – such is the nature of Virgo. Indeed, the son of her, friend Michael Morgan Theis, aged 92 recalled to art director and editor, Sophie Dutton, his memories from when he was a child about being in Gill's home in Plashet Grove. He said: "I remember how everything was quite tickety-boo. Nothing was misplaced in the kitchen, except for a round table where everything was laid out, filled with papers, inks and pens – whatever she was working on" (Dutton, 2019, M.M.T. in conversation with Dutton). He also recalled how Gill wore "plain frocks, jumper or blouse with her hair down" (ibid). The physical appearance of Gill was also remembered by a former employee of Gill's son who met her several times and who, in 1968, recalled that: "Her eyes were beautiful, being a soft deep brown, large and luminous" (Dutton, 2019, 203).

The aspect Saturn trine the ascendant indicates that Gill may also have given the impression of being controlled and restrained, reserved and serious. For that reason, it was difficult to see what was truly going on inside and beneath Gill's persona. She was also described as "painfully shy to the point of timidity" and "in spite of her delicate appearance, she was a strong person" (Dutton, 2019, 202). This shows what tremendous inner strength Gill possessed and how appearances can be deceptive. She was also described by a neighbour who lived close to her off Plashet Grove who said that she "knew little of her as she was almost a recluse... when I met her, she was reserved but emanated an atmosphere of culture and gentility" (Dutton, 2019, 174).

Saturn is in the ninth house of Gill's natal chart and this suggests that she gave careful thought to her belief system and took philosophy and religion seriously. It also suggests that she may have thought education was important and perhaps this is why, when she was an adult, she was eager to learn about esoteric subjects such as theosophy. It is also believed that she enjoyed classic literature such as John Bunyan's *Pilgrim's Progress* (*Raw Vision*, 2015, Ayad, 30) and Dantés' *Inferno* (Cardinal, 1972, 142), as well as *The Bible* and *The Koran* (*LIGHT*, Vol.140, 19). Born under the traditional sign of Capricorn, progress for Gill may well have meant being a mother, homemaker and wife, which was the norm in the early to mid-1900s for somebody of her background and class.

SKILL, INITIATIVE AND SUCCESS

Mars is in the tenth house – the area which is ruled by Capricorn and Saturn in the natural zodiac (*see glossary*). This position suggests that Gill was capable of taking her own initiative and she could organise herself and others with efficiency. It shows that she was hardworking and, with Mars positioned in Gemini, shows that she could multi-task and liked variety in her work. In medical astrology, the fingers and hands (amongst other areas) are ruled by Gemini. This suggests that Gill could be dexterous with her hands and needed to 'keep them busy.' Mars in Gemini also shows that she had determination and the strength to assert herself in order to complete her tasks. Interestingly, one of Gill's untitled ink on postcards, held at the London Borough of Newham Heritage and Archives, shows the word 'Mars' written in large black letters (Dutton, 2019, 166). It is undated but possibly it was drawn during the First or Second World War and is pertinent to both conflicts, as other associations of Mars include hostilities and war. As Gill had astrological knowledge and she would have been aware of the correspondences of Mars.

There is a quincunx aspect created between the Sun and Mars in her natal chart. This indicates an excessive need for action and it is possible that she may have been irritated by those less

Lady in a Hat – postcard art in pen and ink by Madge Gill, with kind permission of Ayshea Ahmed.

efficient and practical than herself, appreciating those who were also skilled with their hands. She must have been impressed and thankful to her son Lawrence therefore, who built her an apparatus on which to produce her larger artistic work in their small home in East Ham.

We can see the want for action through the Mars in Gemini position, whereby Gill produced tremendous pieces of work through using her hands. One example of this can be seen by her creating a piece of art which was 120 feet in size and which was eventually exhibited. We can see the Mars in Gemini at play here again, through her nervous vigour and restlessness, as she literally produced thousands of pieces of artwork. She also created tangible items for more practical purposes through dressmaking, embroidering, knitting and rug-making; showing her capable and resourceful skills.

Her principle artistic success was of the repeated image of feminine figures with hats or headwear with a stereotyped nose and mouth in an oval face with large eyes, often shaded by a hat, and with a bewildered, almost vacant expression. Usually, the female is wearing flowing robed garments where the body is totally covered and only occasionally can one see flesh, such as parts of the lower arms or hands. Equally significant to the female image is the variety of images and symbols, such as circles, cobwebs, crosses, dots, wavy lines and zigzags, as well as chequered patterns, tiled floors and curved arcs as archways; which are enigmatic and almost hypnotic. It is widely believed that Madge never drew any male figures. The publication, *Truth*, described Gill's piece called *Reincarnation*: "It represents a great many figures in an arabesque setting with architectural suggestions and it is carried out with extraordinary skill and feeling" (*LIGHT*, 2019, Vol.140, 48).

The aforementioned Michael Morgan Theis came to know Madge through his mother's long-term friendship with Gill. In an interview with art-director and editor, Sophie Dutton, he recalled how he used to visit Gill at home when he was a child. He remembered seeing her work diligently at her art (Dutton, 2019, interview with M.M. Theis). The first time he visited her at Plashet Grove, he recalled how he was instantly "fascinated by her; the way she would sit at the table with a mug of tea and start drawing in one corner, especially when she was doing the long mural fabrics, she would just go. There didn't seem to be any plan at all" (ibid). He said of Gill: "I was always amazed by the skill and design of what she was working on, whether it was a postcard or a sheet of paper, which all seemed to come from within herself" (ibid).

Whilst visiting Gill and watching her work, Theis said that she didn't talk much and least about herself, "but would often mutter away as she was drawing – to me, it was just background noise; like free-fall talk … she used names of saints that had come to her while she was working" (ibid). The reference about saints 'coming to Gill' as she worked is insightful.

Firstly, she produced (using ink on paper) an image of Joan of Arc (Collection Grosvenor Gallery), who was canonised in 1920 and eventually became patron saint of France. St. Joan (like Gill) was clairaudient (*see glossary*) and clairvoyant (*see glossary*), for which she was persecuted and ridiculed. She credited Saint Catherine of Alexandria and Saint Margaret of Antioch for their divine counsel, which helped her bring victory on the battlefields in the siege of Orléans. She also claimed to have been guided by and had visions of Saint Michael the archangel.

There is another correlation with a saint in Gill's life, that of St. Francis of Assisi. This is because in a passage from *The Holy Converse of Saint Francis*, he being a man of the fervent practice 'Work is Prayer' wrote: "I was ever in the habit of working with mine own hands." He believed that the Church was to be saved by the faith and work of the people (Bayley, 1912, 36). There are certainly echoes here of Gill's faith and belief, perhaps referencing Saint Francis' practice, when she told Dr Boyle in 1922 that she couldn't stop working and declared: "Mine worker's hands" (*Raw Vision*, 2015, 33 / Ayad). Perhaps Gill learnt about Saint Francis of Assisi whilst at the Barnardo's home. His strong work ethic may have inspired her to constantly work hard and in doing so in her belief brought her nearer to 'God'.

RESTLESSNESS AND WILLFULLNESS

Mars is bi-novile (eighty degrees) Uranus in her natal chart. This aspect can suggest a highly-strung nervous system, almost hyperactive with an inability to relax because the mental drive is constant. However, Mars bi-novile also creates a positive energy for when decisive and immediate action is required and shows that Gill could be determined and intractable at times, one example being her wilfulness to return to England from Canada. The energies between Mars and Uranus are also a signal of extremism and the obvious illustration of this can be seen by the tremendous volume of work that she produced. The Newham Local History and Archives have amongst their collection of Gill's

'Lady Standing Up with Netting' – postcard art in pen and ink by Madge Gill. Licensed by London Borough of Newham.

works 26 drawings on postcards in ink, which were all dated by Gill as being created on the 16th January, 1927. Two weeks later, on the 30th January, 1927, she produced eighteen ink drawings on postcards (Newham Local History & Archives, Postcards, Pack F). Clearly, in January of 1927, there was something she wanted to channel through her art and was inspired to create in that month. The volume of work in that month and year is one example of her seemingly going to extremes although, for her, perhaps it was not an extremity. Gill revealed: "My pictures take my mind off the worries" (Dutton, 2019, 11). This shows that working compulsively and often to extremes was her way of trying to escape from her problems and potentially releasing any anxieties and fears she may have had.

Mars provides strength and vitality to push forward and another possibility associated with Mars in the tenth house suggests challenges with authority figures and parent(s), this is because Mars is associated with animosity and conflict. It is possible, therefore, that Gill may have had antagonistic feelings towards those in authority at the Barnardo's Girls Home and the various families that she worked for in Canada as a domestic servant. She may also have felt that she had to prove herself in her life.

Ambition is also indicated with Mars in the tenth house and is illustrated by the following situation. When she was a child living in Canada with her employers the Rae's, although she was treated well there, she left for alternative employment and higher wages. From this, we can see that she had a realistic plan to save money, in order that she could purchase a ticket to return to England. She could have accepted her circumstances in Canada, but didn't. Instead, she used her enterprising spirit to help her return to England. This shows her ambitious and pragmatic drive and is another example of Mars in the tenth house.

Moving away from Mars and turning to her Moon sign; on the day Gill was born, the Moon was in the sign of Aquarius. We can be certain of the sign that the Moon was in as the ephemeris (*see glossary*) shows that the Moon was in that sign all day. What it is less certain however are the aspects created to the Moon. However, the *possible* aspects created with the Moon are significant, as they bear credence to what we know about Gill's life and this will be discussed further on.

DISTICTION AND INDEPENDENCE

The Moon in Aquarius suggests that Gill needed to retain her individuality and experiment with different areas in life. Although she was conventional and habitual in one way, she still needed freedom and space – a message repeated by the various planets in the ninth house of her natal chart. One can see this through her undertaking the role of mother, homemaker and wife, whilst at the same time applying her originality and self-expression through her art, mediumship and practice as a consultant astrologer. These areas made a distinct and unique mark in the outer world and also in her personal life. Her sole-surviving son, Lawrence, told the *Evening Standard* newspaper two years after she died: "I have always believed my mother to be a genius" (Dutton, 2019, 174).

At times, Gill may have seemed distant and unfeeling. This is because Aquarius is ruled by the air element, which is associated with logic and reasoning. Intellectually however, it shows that Gill could be stimulating, and this is further emphasised by Mercury also being in Aquarius. This position shows that she had a bright and progressive mind, perhaps in some ways it made her ahead of her time. She has, as we already know, been described by some as a genius. This illustrates the position of Mercury in Aquarius perfectly. Equally though, Gill may have been misunderstood, perhaps even considered eccentric and strange by others less enlightened or understanding of her nature.

Originality and innovation were important to Gill. She recognised her artistic gifts and the originality of her vision(s), for she wrote: "Deep down in the heart of every human being there lies the soul with its longing, yearning after the attainable, but at what a cost to the unrecognised individual who strikes out after originality?" (Cardinal, 1972, 145). Through her inspiration, Gill did indeed create a distinct and remarkable style of her own – enigmatic and mystifying even to this day. Roger Cardinal believed that by placing her emotions in the objective space of her pictures, it allowed her to escape from the "drab existence in which she found herself" (ibid). Perhaps he was right.

The Moon in Aquarius also indicates how Gill was inspired and motivated by independent and liberated women. For example, her friend the journalist, Louise Morgan, was a feminist (Dutton, 2019, interview with M.M. Theis) and, as previously discussed, Dr Alice Helen Anne Boyle was a pioneer in her field and the first female president of the Royal Medico Psychological Association, not forgetting Madame Helena Petrovna Blavatsky who founded The Theosophical Society in 1875 and which, as we know, Gill became a member in the 1920s.

Gill may also have been aware that, in the 1920s, artist and suffragette, Sylvia Pankhurst, moved to Charteris Road in Woodford Green, Essex. She lived there with her boyfriend, Silvio Corio, who was an Italian anarchist. Pankhurst set up the East London Federation of the Suffragettes in Bow; this was an offshoot of the Women's Social and Political Union. It was a vocal advocate not only for the vote but also for the rights of the working classes. When Pankhurst and Corio moved to twee Woodford Green, it caused outrage at the time. Not only because of Pankhurst's politics, but also because she was living out of wedlock with her partner. Interestingly, Charteris Road was a short bus ride away from where Gill lived in 1919, in George Lane, South Woodford. It seems that Gill was more than aware of the inequalities between the sexes economically, politically and socially. When she was approximately 30, she said: "If I had been a man I would have gone abroad & studied botany, Himalayan rare flowers" (www.newhamheritagemonth.org).

Aside from the imbalance of opportunity for Gill due to her class and gender, the aforementioned statement also shows that she was interested in other cultures, was eager to learn and had knowledge of horticulture. Gill may have learnt about the Himalayan rare flowers through her studies of theosophy, as Madame Blavatsky also wrote extensively about her travels in India.

As Gill had astrological knowledge, she would have known about some of the correspondences associated with her Sun sign, Capricorn. One example being that some astrologers believe that India is one of the countries associated with Capricorn (Parkers, 1991, 119). The connection with Capricorn and India may be considered because of the caste system and tradition, which is in keeping with the hierarchy and rules associated with Capricorn. It is notable that India is associated with Capricorn, especially given that Gill was thought to speak Hindustani.

Today, modern India's huge population is diverse as well as devout, and most of the world's Hindus, Jains and Sikhs live in India. It is also home to one of the world's largest Muslim populations and to millions of Christians and Buddhists (www.pewresearch.org). As noted earlier, Buddhism is a practice used by many theosophists and Madame Blavatsky had strong spiritual connections with Tibet in East Asia. Interestingly, one of Gill's pen and ink postcard drawing is called *Children of the East*.

Returning to the symbolism of the Moon in Aquarius again; the position suggests that there may have been challenges in Gill's early life, especially with attachment in relationships. This is certainly borne out in her formative years. Previously, she had been moved from one care giver to another. Her first sense of security that she experienced was probably with the Dr Barnardo's orphanage, as she was there for several years before they sent her abroad – this may have been her first sense of 'family'. Gill may have felt at times that there was no permanence or stability in her life and may have found it difficult to form close relationships with others, especially as a child.

CULTURE, PHILOSOPHY AND RELIGION

Moving on to the sign of Sagittarius on the IC; this position suggests that Gill may have felt like a 'foreigner' in the aforementioned 'home-settings' and this is due to this sign being associated with different cultures. However, it also suggests that Gill had a large family, as Sagittarius and its ruler, Jupiter, are associated with expanse and vastness. Indeed, Madge Gill did have an extensive family. This was borne out in her life by way of being a fostered child and then living in an orphanage with a wide range of children and various 'mother figures' employed there.

By being sent to Canada, we can see the overseas Sagittarius/Jupiter connection of her being in a new country with a different culture. She may have met other races and experienced different religions whilst she was there. Faith and religion are also associated with Sagittarius and its ruler, Jupiter. Therefore, it is noteworthy that her mother's family were based at the Central Synagogue in London when she was born, although it appears the family did not practice Judaism. Qualities of self-righteousness, being moralistic and opinionated are some of the less attractive characteristics of Sagittarius. Gill may have experienced these areas through her various 'family figures' growing-up. However, as this sign is also associated with exploration and freedom, we know that as an adult Gill ventured into other areas of religion such as spiritualism, which then was unorthodox and progressive.

Children at the Barnardo's homes were issued with a Bible and prayer book and they took these with them in their trunks when they sailed to Canada (www.canadianbritishhomechildren.weebly.com). From these early examples in her life, we can see the religious element of the Sagittarius IC at play. Thomas Barnardo built his charity upon biblical foundations and the children received religious education and learnt the Bible at the Barnardo's Village for Girls where there was also a church. Faith and religion were significant to Gill throughout her life and this theme is echoed by the stellium of planets seen in the ninth house of her natal chart – the area associated with belief, faith, morals, religion and philosophy.

Examples of this are borne out by her membership of The Theosophy Society when she was in her early forties and where she would have been encouraged to study comparative religions (such as Brahmanism and Buddhism), philosophy, as well as investigating the unexplained laws of nature and the powers latent within each individual. We know that she was a spiritualist and also held belief in God and Christ and the Saints (Dutton, 2019, M.M.T. on interview sheet). At the Lady Chichester

Hospital, there was a secular chapel that patients could use; whether Gill used it is unknown but it is plausible, given her widely held beliefs.

When she was in her late fifties, Gill lived near spiritualist churches. For example, when she lived at Thorngrove Road in Upton Park, she would have been fairly near to Plaistow Spiritualist Church. In 1940, when Gill lived at Plashet Grove in Upton Park, her closest churches would have been Manor Park Spiritualist Church (still active and founded 1906) which is on Shrewsbury Road, Forest Gate; and Little Ilford Spiritualist Church (founded in 1925 and still active) on Third Avenue, Manor Park (Archivist at Newham Archives Centre in correspondence to Author). It is believed that she exhibited one of her paintings, *Moses in the Bulrushes*, at one of the spiritualist churches (*LIGHT*, June, 2019, 33) but it is unknown which church.

Gill was also clairaudient, as previously noted, and one example of this can be seen with what she told Dr Boyle and which Boyle recorded in her consultation notes. Gill told Dr Boyle that God had told her to write a book of Jewish rites, which she did. Gill wrote approximately 50 books, but then burnt or tore many of them up. She continued to tell Dr Boyle that "God's eyes were all around her room, watching her, and he said: 'What are you doing tearing up all my work? You will have to write it out again!" (Dutton, 2019, 108). Mercury in Aquarius is also an indicator of an alert mind and open-mindedness, as well as being innovative even groundbreaking. Certainly, we can see how broad-minded Gill was when it came to religion. This is borne out by her sustaining her Christian upbringing that she had grown-up with at Barnardo's (and in Canada), whilst later embracing other religions such as Hinduism and spiritualism.

After Gill's death, a newspaper reporter aptly wrote about Gill: "It is almost a tradition in art for painters to die before their genius is recognised" (Dutton, 2029, 173/*Stratford* Express, 18/10/1963). Her friend, Michael Morgan Theis, said of her:

"She was unique and had her own stamp on everything she did. I never felt Madge Gill's work was weird. I was fascinated by it – there was a bit of magic to it, you couldn't help but ask where it all came from" (Dutton, 2019, M.M. Theis interview).

BEING AN OUTSIDER ARTIST

Uranus, the ruler of Aquarius, is positioned in the first house – the area which governs appearance and presentation. This suggests that Gill may have been considered as odd, especially if she had an unusual appearance. One example of this is borne out by her left glass eye that she had as an adult. During the 1920s, wearing a glass eye was apparent and not as subtle as it is today – so children, for example, may have been shocked and unsettled by her impediment at an initial glance.

She certainly had a distinct style through her own dressmaking and she also used colours, fabrics and materials that others may have thought unconventional at the time, such as dresses made from balloon material and wools of different colour. After Gill died, newspaper reporter, David Rallis, wrote: "… some of the colours that she used are very fashionable today but were quite daring in the1930s" (Dutton, 2019, 175). This shows how courageous and experimental she was, as well as being alternative in her self-expression.

It is interesting that Gill became known as an 'Outsider Artist' after she died. This is because Aquarius' characteristics include being unorthodox and 'on the edge', which is certainly pertinent to Gill. This is because Outsider Artists were defined as individuals who freely created art without any thought for an audience to view their work, they were innovative and unique. English pop artist, Sir Peter Blake, observed that, "quite often outsider artists are on their own and quite often they're melancholic" (Dutton, 2019, Peter Blake interview), he continued that for Madge Gill, art was the one thing she had that she could focus on (ibid).

As discussed earlier, the Moon can indicate qualities about one's caretaker or parent. Often it is the mother, but not always, depending on an individual's situation. It is also associated with one's early experiences in life. Aquarius is also associated with communities and groups, so it is interesting knowing that Gill was raised by various people and potentially this may have made her feel different or unwanted. More so as Aquarius and its ruler, Uranus, are also associated with distance and space, it is significant that Gill was separated from her mother Emma and then fostered by the Leakey family and, as far as we know, she rarely, if ever, saw her mother again. However, Emma was permitted to see her grandsons and did so when she lived in Woodford with her family (www.madgegill.com). As previously discussed, Emma Elizabeth Eades was considered an 'outsider', in as much that her own family and society thought her shameful for having an illegitimate child and for having learning difficulties and mental health issues.

FEELINGS AND NURTURING

Returning again to Gill's astrology and three of the Moon's potential aspects which comprise of: the Moon conjunct Mercury, the Moon square Saturn, and the Moon trine Pluto. The Moon conjunct Mercury suggests that Gill may have rationalised her feelings with common practical sense and tempered situations with hard facts. One example of this can be seen by the following. Upon her return from Canada and many years later, in a letter to a friend she wrote: "I was in Canada as a child from twelve years old 'til nineteen. What memories I have left behind" (Dutton, 2019, 37). One can only speculate as to what she meant by that. It could literally mean that she couldn't remember anything from her time in Canada, or that what she did remember she wanted to forget because it was too painful for her when she recalled it. The Director of British Home Children, Advocacy and Research

Association, Lori Oschefski, said that "It is a very common trait in the BHC that they (children) would become introverted and would not speak of their past and even admit or have it known that they were BHC" (Dutton, 2019, 42).

Perhaps this was why Gill broke with her past and called herself Madge when she returned from Canada, keeping that name throughout her lifetime. Oschefski continued that the BHC's introversion may have stemmed in some cases from the abuse they may have experienced, as well as a deep sense of shame from constantly being treated and told that they were unwanted and unworthy (ibid). There doesn't appear to be anything documented about Gill being ill-treated but that doesn't mean that it didn't happen.

The Moon square Saturn aspect suggests that Gill was emotionally self-sufficient and may have expressed her feelings with caution and controlled responses. It also suggests that she craved security and a family which could provide her with protection and feelings of safety, as a child she may have even felt abandoned and unloved. If she did, it would be understandable, given her fragmented early years. The Moon trine Pluto suggests that she could bury her feelings deeply, especially any feelings to do with hurt and pain. If this was true of Gill, she may have buried and channelled them through her arts and crafts, which may have helped towards a healing process for her.

The trine aspect between the Moon and Pluto also indicates that Gill could cope in any domestic crisis and that she could transform a situation using her insight and nurturing qualities. These merits would have made her an effective nurse, as well as a determined and nurturing mother at critical times of need. One obvious example of her inner strength and resilience is when she cared for her son, who had been injured in a motorbike accident. He was bed-bound and disabled for two or three years until he recovered. Gill had sat at his bedside for long periods of time, often right through the night during his period of illness and she was determined that her son should heal and recover. One wonders if Gill would have remained in nursing had she not married her husband and had children.

Another interpretation of the Moon trine Pluto aspect is that Gill was intuitive and perceptive to any moods or undercurrents. One example of this is illustrated by what she told Dr Boyle when she was under her care in the hospital in Hove. The doctor's notes recorded that Gill, when talking about her inspired painted pictures, told Boyle that "They are all around her room at home – and that you can see at once that they are divine – you can feel the sacredness of the atmosphere as soon as you open the door" (*The Keep,* East Sussex Archives, Medical Report, 2–3). This shows how she was receptive to different types of energies and had a well-developed sixth sense.

Another example connected to her feelings and sensitivity can be seen through her comments in *The Prediction* magazine interview in 1937, when she was 55. She emphatically outlined that when she was compelled to draw on a large scale on calico "I simply couldn't leave off ... All the time I was in quite a normal state of mind and there was no suggestion of any 'spirit' standing beside me. I simply felt inspired" (*LIGHT,* 2019, Vol.140, 172). This suggests that she must have had experience(s) of 'spirits' standing next to her at some stage in her life to know the difference between inspiration and spirit contact. Interestingly, a newspaper commented on her work when it was exhibited in 1938 that it was "made with an obvious passion" showing how the compulsion and obsession was evident in her art (https://www.academia.edu). The preponderance of the fixed mode in her natal chart shows her cast-iron will and determination to complete her artistic task.

Returning again to the emotionality connected with the Moon trine Pluto aspect and how it manifested in her life; areas of loss and rejection were considerable through most of Gill's life and she had tremendous resilience in rising above situations, irrespective of any deep emotional pain. One could say that she was rejected by Victorian society for being illegitimate; in addition, she never had the love of both parents. She lost her mother as a child and was fostered by another family, then she was rejected by them and had to be placed in a Barnardo's home for girls. Next, and as previously discussed, she was forced to sail to Canada and work for various families as part of the British Home Children programme.

COMMUNICATION, MERCURY AND VARIETY

The MC is Gemini in her natal chart and the ruler of Gemini is Mercury, which also rules Virgo – her ascendant sign. The MC Gemini suggests having potential to succeed in the field of communication, as well as being greatly stimulated by having a range of tasks to undertake in her daily life or any vocational calling.

A talent for languages is also conducive to the MC Gemini. Mercury is known in Roman mythology as the Messenger God, the Winged Messenger, and certainly Gill regarded herself as a messenger of God, which can be seen in her medical notes from Dr Boyle. Gill was a communicator by way of her producing automatic writing, clairvoyant messages, communicating information through her artwork, as well as speaking other languages, although she did not know what languages they were (this will be discussed further on in more detail). She said of her rapidly drawn pictures that she can hardly understand them but believes they hold the key to the world's progress. (*LIGHT*, 2019, Vol.140, 25). Harry Edwards wrote of mediums that were able to produce inspirational writing that they are understandably proud of it. He observed that, "Often the theme is of a theological character, pointing out the way of right living, and the medium desires that others may profit from the teachings" (Edwards, 2003, 33). This is certainly true of Gill and her desire for the purposes of progress in humanity.

This was another example of her way of communicating and whilst she said that she couldn't understand the pictures themselves, she instinctively felt the languages she spoke and wrote were to better humanity. She told a *Sunday Express* reporter in 1922 that her spirit-guide informed her that when the languages are interpreted it "will prepare the world for the dawn of a new era in civilisation" (*LIGHT*, 2019, Vol.140, 25). Perhaps this is referring to humanity currently being at the dawning of the Age of Aquarius. Certainly, there has been tremendous Aquarian progress made already through the developments of human rights and technological advancements. Currently, we are still living in the Age of Pisces, which started approximately at the time of the birth of Christ.

Gill also claimed to the unnamed *Sunday Express* reporter that when her spirit-guide makes his visitations, he does not confine himself to one language and the variety of languages used "become so confused that their interpretation is impossible" (ibid). This suggests that Gill had made some attempts herself to interpret the various languages, which shows her curious and hard-working nature. It also shows some of the Gemini MC of her natal chart in action, by way of assimilation, curiosity, languages, translation as well as learning, speaking and writing.

Given that her spirit-guide visited her for many years, we can see how significantly the Gemini/Mercury associations manifested in her life, as well as the Mercury in Aquarius position and Mercury square Neptune aspect in her natal chart, which will be discussed in more detail further on. Thus far, her automatic writing has not been interpreted, although Gill made attempts to appeal to experts to try and help her understand it. For example, in 1922, she wrote to a Sir David Ross of the Oriental School of Languages (ibid) in London. Presumably, it was a fruitless attempt, as we know nothing about his response to Gill, if indeed he ever did reply to her.

It has been observed by astrologer, Demian Allan, that there is evidence of the occult Enochian language (*see glossary*) in

Gill's automatic writing (*LIGHT*, 2019, Vol.140, 29). This ancient language was founded by astrologer and occultist, Dr John Dee, in the sixteenth century with the assistance of the medium and seer Edward Kelley, and indicates application of ancient script(s) in her work.

During the Renaissance period, magicians were keen to understand what happened in the Garden of Eden and the Fall of Man. They perceived that this could only be possible by contact with the angels and that they (the angels) used a special kind of alphabetic script to do so. The magicians designated these scripts as Angelic/Adamic or Celestial; claiming they were representative of the original language and alphabet of pre-Flood man or the Adama (*see glossary*) (M.B. Jackson in correspondence to Author).

Gill's son, Lawrence, observed just how varied his mother's drawings were and included figures such as Moses in the bulrushes, Deborah, Jacob, Noah and the Flood (*LIGHT*, 2019, Vol.140, 19), all of whom are figures from *The Book of Genesis*, the first book of *The Hebrew Bible* and the *Christian Old Testament*. Other figures in her work included several of the prophets and sages (ibid) and some of Gill's newspaper interviews and works reference the Garden of Eden.

Returning again to the astrology of Gill's natal chart; there is an angle made between the ascendant and MC which is just out of orb of being a square. This indicates an emphasis on Gill's communicative and intellectual faculties, her adaptable and curious nature, as well as a great ability to work hard; especially in any area which required control of detail and minutia. Obvious examples of this are her works of art in coloured and black inks which have intricate patterns and formations in them. Her other skill of embroidery would have required manipulation of the needle to apply thread or yarn to decorate fabric or other materials. She improvised her own techniques for applying colour schemes and patterns. Gill made dresses for herself as well as rugs, showing the practical and resourceful side of her skills. She was a talented seamstress and was first employed in this position when she returned from Canada; this, again, would have required careful and detailed work.

Mercury, as previously noted, is positioned in the fifth house and indicates that she had a talent for writing, as well as having a bright and lively mind. One obvious example of this is through her automatic writing using pen and ink on paper, as well as her poetical gifts. An illustration of this can be seen through her verse written on postcard in pen and ink: "The clouds will burst and the Sun will shine again" (Dutton, 2019, 246, from Collection at the Henry Boxer Gallery). Gill's letter writing to her friends "often included illustrated postcards and photographs of her work within the correspondence" (Dutton, 2019, 179).

CHILDREN AND CREATIVITY

As the fifth house is associated with children and childhood, we can use this area to observe some qualities of her sons and also Gill's attitude towards them. From the position of the Moon in Aquarius in the fifth house, there is symbolism that she wanted children. She had the ability to nurture them as friends and positively encourage their creative talents, taking pleasure from their achievements; this is also indicated by Venus being positioned in the fifth house. One example is a handwritten poem written by her first son, Leonard Eric Gill, known as 'Bob' (Dutton, 2019, 148) called *The Darkened Night*. Exactly how old he was when he wrote this poem is unknown but it is the handwriting of a young boy and is dedicated to his mother. The poem is now in the Grosvenor Gallery Collection (ibid). Clearly, Gill cherished her son's poem as she kept it all her life.

Less known is that, like their mother, Lawrence and Leonard Gill also exhibited their own artwork for the East End Academy at the Whitechapel Gallery. This was in 1932 and 1934. The *East End Advertiser* newspaper editorial on the 4th November, 1932, reported: "Laurence (sic) J. Gill and Leonard Gill, both have ink drawings hanging. The latter's drawings are somewhat like those of his mother, but Laurence is more architectural in his designs" (https://www.academia.edu). Perhaps all three of them encouraged each other to exhibit for the East End Academy but more likely her son (Lawrence) encouraged her to exhibit. Interestingly, we can see the practical nature of Madge Gill at play by the following information reported by *The Daily Herald* which said: "She looked in the day before the private view opened and she said 'I've only come to see if they look patchy'" (ibid). This shows not only her attitude towards the practicalities of her art but also that she took pride in her work, wanting it to appear the best that it could be. In the catalogue for that exhibition, Madge's art was described as: "Three 36 feet long pen and ink drawings of mystic subjects," followed by: "The artist Madge Gill, described as an umbrella-mender's mother" (ibid).

Gill's eldest son, Lawrence (also known as 'Laurie'), enjoyed writing and also encouraged his mother's talents. Aged 25, he wrote a broadsheet (Collection of The College of Psychic Studies, London) titled "'*Myrninerest. The Spheres*' – it was the first edition and priced at one shilling" (Dutton, 2019, 67). In it he explains what inspiration is and draws upon his mother's spiritual abilities and experiences and how her artwork was worthy of consideration. It is believed to have been written to vent his frustration about his mother's works being rejected by the (then) librarian of the London Spiritualist Alliance, Mercy Phillimore (*LIGHT*, Vol.140, Special Edition, 41). This would have been the second time that his mother's work was rejected; the first time being by the Psychical Research Society. One wonders if there was an unconscious bias towards Madge Gill for being a working class, East End housewife and mother.

Lawrence had previously offered some of his mother's work to the Alliance to be exhibited but it was rejected for reasons unknown (ibid). Lawrence had written to the organisation after his mother had success when her work was showcased in Belgium. Presumably, Lawrence was enthused by this. When his mother's artwork was rejected by the organisation, he felt exceptionally disappointed and vented his feeling through writing.

Aside from enjoying writing, Lawrence apparently was also a "brilliant pianist" (Dutton, 2019, 174). Gill also claimed that her son (son unnamed but possibly Lawrence) liked to write fairy stories. She also observed that both of her sons were clairvoyant (The Keep, East Sussex Records, Gill's Medical Records, 6). Lawrence was definite that his mother's work would come into the spotlight with some acclaim and told an employee of his (he owned a small umbrella business in Green Street) in the mid-1950s, that his mother's artwork would be recognised after her death (Dutton, 2019, 203). These turned out to be prophetic words. Clearly, her sons had inherited some of their mother's gifts and their abilities were supported and understood by their mother – something not afforded to Gill as a child. As previously noted, Gill claimed she had "seen things all her life" (Dutton, 2019, 108 / Ayad).

It seems that Gill was kind, not only to her own sons but also to her neighbour's children. Teenager, John Tutteitt (her neighbour's son), told an *Evening Standard* newspaper journalist in 1963, after her death, how, when he was much younger, she was kind to him and the other children that he played with outside in Plashet Grove. He said that Mrs Gill used to come out of her house and give us children money for sweets and ice-creams. He continued that she was very generous but would never speak when she gave us the money (Dutton, 2019, 174). Perhaps she was treating the children as she would have liked to be treated in her own childhood.

MIND MATTERS AND PSYCHIC ABILITY

Two aspects made with Mercury in Gill's natal chart comprise of Mercury square Saturn, and Mercury square Neptune. The Mercury square Saturn aspect would have helped Gill to concentrate and keep a disciplined mind, preventing her from getting distracted and making her able to complete any task. This is certainly borne out in her determination to complete any of her textiles and pictures, however extensive the task was. This aspect is also an indicator of significant challenges to overcome; the real challenge is the mind itself. This is because the energy of Saturn inhibits and restricts and also generates serious-thinking.

One example of this is borne out by her attitude and respect towards her spirit-guide, who demanded that she wrote volumes of Jewish rites. Perhaps other areas of her life were sacrificed because of the sheer amount of time given to her spiritual obligations.

Mercury square Saturn also indicates potential for negative thinking which can be exacerbated by having to deal with a lot of responsibility or suffering through painful hardships, separations and losses. Other themes connected with this area include isolation and loneliness, which can lead to depression. However, Saturn also brings qualities of coping strategies, as well as endurance.

As we have already seen through Gill's biographical information, these areas were borne out throughout her life. Despite all her challenges and hardships; it was her belief, faith and a philosophical outlook which helped her to survive any crisis and painful difficulties, be they emotional or physical. In a letter to her friend, journalist Louise Morgan, she told her: "All my life I have had to fight for principals if they count for anything! Yet I dwell in a world of disalusion" (sic) (Dutton, 2019, 178). This shows some of Gill's disappointments and frustrations in her life. Her artistic creativity was surely an outlet for her pain and inevitably helped her to try and heal.

Turning now to the Mercury square Neptune aspect in Gill's natal chart and how it is pertinent to what we know of Gill. Like all aspects, there are many possibilities and variations as to how Mercury square Neptune played out in her life. Firstly, it suggests that she saw and sensed the world through a different lens to anybody else, i.e. not the factual or real world. Obvious examples of this are through her psychic and mediumistic abilities. Whilst she was in the Lady Chichester Hospital, she told Dr Boyle that she had heard and seen things for as long as she could remember (Dutton, 2019, 108 / Ayad).

This may add weight as to why Gill, as a child, was referred to in the following way: "There came to a time when the family decided it could no longer cope with this embarrassing child and, even though her mother was still alive, the nine year old was committed to Dr Barnardo's" (www.madgegill.com). If she was able to see and hear spirit activity that her family could not, this may have been of concern to them. As far as we know, the Eades family were not gifted in this sense and so it must have been bewildering for them and possibly also Gill as a young child; although it may have been the norm for Gill.

When she was interviewed for *The Prediction* magazine in 1937, she told the interviewer that whilst she was working with fabric the material itself was covered with 'lights' and that her room at night is illuminated with various colours and hues, especially gold. Outside of her room, there would be sheets of colour of light (*LIGHT*, Vol.140, June 2019, 172). This is another example of her being able to see things with a clairvoyant and psychic eye. Her embroidery and tapestry work were certainly a colourful and vibrant contrast to much of her pen and ink postcard works. Perhaps, whilst she was working with various colours, she was able to process and receive 'messages' (associated with Mercury), which was why she became semi-entranced through her sensitivity, which enabled her to work 'automatically'.

Her clairvoyant and psychic abilities may have had adverse effects on her relationships, by being misunderstood by others. For example, when Gill was an adult and first saw her guide, 'the high priest', her immediate family were concerned about her mental well-being. They took her to see a mental specialist who in fact pronounced her perfectly sane (Dutton, 2019, 114). From this example, we can see that her own family did not have the understanding of Gill's talents, nor of spiritualism, and it caused concern and bewilderment.

Author, Colin Rhodes, believed that "spiritualism afforded Madge Gill a structure that promised inclusion as well as support for her intense emotional pain" (Rhodes, 2000, 147). This appears to be the case for many people who, aside from personal grief, had also lived through the First World War (including the influenza pandemic of 1918) and lived with all the consequences that it brought. These major events upon humanity, as well as the many missing people during the war, were contributing factors for the rise in popularity of spiritualism, as did the building of spiritualist churches and home-circles. Rhodes claimed that "Gill had long been in contact with spiritualist circles and, as a direct result of trying to contact her dead children on the other side, a succession of creative activities began" (Rhodes, 2000, 149).

WORKING WITH SPIRIT ENERGY

Bert (her brother-in-law) and Aunt Kate were both still alive when Gill was (as she termed it) *'possessed'* by her spirit-guide. It seems odd that they were unable to assist Mr Gill and his sons with his wife's experience. It is believed that her Aunt Kate was a spiritualist and should have known about the importance of 'opening and closing safely' – meaning using prayer and/or meditation when working with spirit. Perhaps Bert and Aunt Kate were never informed or taught about this important preparation, although, upon reflection, it does seem unlikely. It is possible that none of the three had ever experienced or seen this kind of 'possession' before; neither did they know how to manage it effectively and safely.

If Gill was not used to appropriate and healthy practice when working with spirit energy then it may have been a contributing factor to the state of her mental health, by not being able to 'close down' or recognise the importance of protecting oneself from 'possession'. Harry Edwards provided sound advice when he wrote: "Be master of the mediumship – do not let it master you … do not allow the guide to come close, unless invited to do so" (Edwards, 2003, 37). His counsel provides good solid advice about keeping the balance when working with spirit energies in mediumship and remaining grounded.

Author and occultist, Dion Fortune, who was also mediumistic and served at spiritualist churches and halls, wrote about the aforementioned subject as well; upon the important matter of not becoming preoccupied with spirit-working – this was in order to remain healthy and balanced. Nutritional diets with plenty of water and quality sleep are crucial for everybody but particularly mediums, if they are to work as effectively as possible. We already know that before Gill was admitted into the Lady Chichester Hospital, she was living with insomnia and not eating the meals her husband had prepared for her. This would not have helped the vitality of her mind, body and spirit. It is also important to remember that many other families were poor and there remained food rationing in the country; this began during the First World War and it continued until 1920. This may have been a contributing factor to Gill being underweight, as observed by Dr Boyle when Gill was in her care in 1922.

One cannot help but wonder if Gill's psychic abilities (as well as her personal traumas) played a contributing part in her marriage breakdown, especially if Thomas Gill had no interest or understanding in esoteric subjects or spiritualism and at times may have treated his wife with indifference. A close friend of

Gill's, a Mrs Fant, reported to journalist, Paula James, that Gill and her husband were separated (Dutton, 2019, 206). Whether this was true is unknown. There appears to be no reference to Thomas Gill by his wife before his death in 1933, at least not in any of the magazine or newspaper articles. Possibly, he stipulated to his wife and sons that he did not want his name connected with her artistic and spiritualist interests. Equally, perhaps she did not want him associated with her interests and talents – nobody really knows.

As a child, Gill may have developed insecurities of a mental or nervous nature (associations of Mercury) and, if so, may have relied on fantasies and her imagination (associations of Neptune) in order to cope – one possibility being that of creating a 'fantasy friend' but also seeing 'spirit friends' from an early age. It would have been helpful and stimulating for Gill to have like-minded, artistic and spiritual people around her for company, who could understand her needs and sensitivities. Certainly, she had that when she lived with her brother-in-law and Aunt Kate when they were alive. She must have missed their stimulating and understanding company after they died.

In astrology, Neptune has many associations (like all the planets) – one being alcohol, and it is long known and advised for mediums to avoid dependency upon it. This is because it can exacerbate one's sensitivities, as well as deplete one's energies – potentially blocking 'messages' coming through for some mediums. It has been said that in her later life, Gill "took to drinking heavily and had a certain reputation in her neighbourhood as a nice old lady when sober, but a terrible woman when drunk" (Cardinal, 1972, 138). Apparently, she was considered a crank and she helped to exacerbate this by "looking people straight in the eye and rattling off a spontaneous prediction that, in some cases, would come true" (ibid).

Perhaps this was one of the reasons why some of her neighbours were wary of her – because of the accuracy of her psychic messages, as well as her unpredictable disposition. Psychic messages can be spontaneous but there is an element of responsibility in how the medium delivers the information (meaning how the message is conveyed and whether the recipient is even ready to accept the message). Clearly, Gill was being irresponsible if she was drunk and spouting predictions randomly at her neighbours. A letter from L.H. Bevan to journalist, Paula James, in 1968 (Dutton, 2019, 204) reflects that once, as a child, he stayed with his parents at their friend's (the Fants) and that same weekend Gill had visited them too (in 1930). Bevan continued that Gill "caused considerable consternation by talking to my parents about a dead relation whom she could not apparently have known previously" (ibid). This shows that, although Gill was an accurate medium, her messages were not always enthusiastically welcomed, especially by those who were not of a spiritualist ilk.

Mrs Fant, the aforementioned friend of Gill, also told James (after Gill had died) that she was "an alcoholic, drank spirits (sic) early on and then later on Guinness" (ibid). She also claimed that Gill was "never a very happy woman, tragic, hated men but not her sons" (ibid). She continued that her friend "could talk for hours. Always thought her drawings were important. 'One of these days ...' she used to say. They will be well thought of" (ibid). From this last piece of information, we can see Gill's foresight came to fruition. Her clairvoyant abilities were also evidenced to Paula James by a bricklayer called William Armstrong. He knew Gill when he did some work for her in 1948. He wrote to James about how he "was astonished by her psychic powers." Gill correctly told him his date of birth and that he had experienced trouble in November; which was true. She also told him that he would never have a lot of money, but "you'll never have any trouble" (Dutton, 2019, 206).

Mercury is connected with communication and skill, as previously discussed, whilst Neptune is associated with art, music, poetry and writing, as well as mediumship and spirituality

– Gill had talents in all of these areas. The Mercury square Neptune aspect indicates that Gill could express herself using her creative talents and vivid imagination. In 1937, when she gave the interview to a representative of *The Prediction* magazine, she told them it was in 1919 that she first started her work (although it was probably 1920, as earlier observed). Continuing, she said: "I then had an inspiration to take up my pen and do all kinds of work of an artistic type. I felt that I had an artistic faculty seeking expression" (*LIGHT*, 2019, Vol.140, 47). In her life, she went on to channel her artistry through crafts, producing knitting (sometimes knitting without patterns and occasionally using only one needle), stitching and weaving, followed by inspirational writings (mostly biblical) (bid), playing the piano, writing and drawing creations with tremendous speed, whilst in a trance-like state (*LIGHT*, 2019, Vol.140, 29).

BELIEF, CALLING, FREEDOM AND TRUTH

Jupiter is conjunct Neptune in her natal chart and suggests that Gill had mystical and religious yearnings and had a great understanding of ethereal subjects; one example of her belief being that God is infinite and has many guises and names. The aspect between Jupiter and Neptune also shows that Gill yearned to work towards a higher order of reality and that through religion and mysticism she was able to escape from the harsh realities of her life (which, as we know, included many disappointments and sorrows) and in doing so also gave her a sense of escape and freedom.

The theme of freedom is further emphasised by the Jupiter trine Uranus aspect, as both are associated with autonomy and independence. This aspect also shows that Gill needed to find meaning and truth in her life, using unorthodox channels in which to find it – one example being astrology. It is also an indication that Gill was interested in different people and their cultures, which can be seen through her work.

Associations of Jupiter include moralising and preaching, whilst some correspondences of Uranus include truthfulness and wilfulness – both are connected with forthrightness. Therefore, Gill may have needed to observe that what was her own truth was not necessarily other people's truth, so she had the potential to be fanatical. This message is also emphasised by Jupiter in the ninth house, which indicates a high moral code. The position shows that Gill had a philosophical, spiritual and positive outlook on life (irrespective of the intense trauma that she had been through) and probably believed that her faith and God would help her to survive challenges in her life. Neptune and Pluto are also in the ninth house in her natal chart. This shows us, once again, that Gill searched for enlightenment through mystical channels and practices such as meditation and prayer, and these would have been of comfort and help to her. It echoes the message that she was searching for answers to the deep and philosophical questions of life, for example: 'why am I here?' and 'what is the meaning of life?'

Pluto in the ninth house also indicates that any crises she experienced in her life may have prompted profound thinking to change or reformulate her life philosophies and moral standards. This shows adaptability and courage in being unafraid to discard outlived values and beliefs. For example, from what we know of her early childhood and the religious element of her Barnardo's upbringing, she changed this by exploring other philosophies and religions such as Buddhism, spiritualism and theosophy.

Chiron the Wounded Healer (*see glossary*) is also in the ninth house. This shows that the driving force in Gill's nature was likely to be of a religious disposition. It also suggests that, early on in her life, whatever religious framework she inherited was not compatible with her inner needs and provided no spiritual nourishment for her. Consequently, finding her meaning and purpose to life may have been a long and lonely road travelled. As previously discussed, the ninth house is associated with foreign cultures and, as we know, Gill lived in Canada as a child until she was a teenager. It is possible that at that time her own beliefs set her apart from others and she may have felt persecuted for holding a different faith. For example, if her employers followed an organised and orthodox religion and Gill told them about any psychic experiences she was having whilst living in their home, they may have been damming and dismissive of her, perhaps even shocked if they were not open to the subject of psychic phenomena and spirits.

We know that Gill had considerable astrological knowledge and may well have been aware of the astrological data of the Moon's Nodes which in her own natal chart comprises of the North Node in Sagittarius and the South Node in Gemini. This symbolises that Gill was being 'called' to embrace a higher life or faith; putting to good use all that she had previously learnt, developing and expanding her knowledge so that she could teach others. She achieved this to an extent whereby in her family she was able to impress upon her sons and (posthumously) on other generations. This was achieved through both her epiphany and her spiritual art – demonstrating that there was more to life than the material world and that one's inner life was as important as the mundane outer one.

Chiron is in Taurus in Gill's natal chart, which indicates one's values, as well as what provides us with a sense of safety and solidarity (Reinhart, 1989, 107). Chiron in Taurus can also be interpreted as one possibly lacking a sense of self-worth, perhaps being unable to value oneself, feeling insecure and insubstantial (ibid). Consequently, one may attach great worth to materialistic possessions as well as finding themselves clinging to people and possessions, hoping to find meaningful substantiality (ibid) where it is lacking in their life.

This is relevant to Gill in what we know about some of her art, where she was offered vast sums of money for her work but she always refused to sell it. This is because she believed that it belonged to Myrninerest, her spirit-guide, and therefore was not hers to sell. Even when she exhibited her work at the Aid for Russia exhibition, she deliberately and excessively over-priced her work, hoping the sum would not generate a sale as she was determined not to sell her work (*LIGHT*, 2019, Vol.140, 2019).

Consequently, she kept many hundreds of pieces of art that she produced, which were found by her son, Lawrence, after she died. Venus, the ruler of Taurus (and Libra), is trine Chiron which indicates that Gill had the gift of seeing beauty where others were oblivious to it, as well as finding value in something that others reject as being ugly or worthless. Astrologer and author, Melanie Reinhart, observed that the "most important relationships in the lives of those with Chiron in aspect to Venus are frequently those which bring artistic inspiration or personal growth, rather than those which lead to marriage or child-rearing" (Reinhart, 1989, 207). This is apt to what little we know about Gill's relationship with her husband.

SATURN APPEARS AS LIFE CLOSES FOR MADGE GILL

When Gill died on 28th January, 1961, there were some interesting astrological progressions (*see glossary*) and transits (*see glossary*) being made to the planets in her natal chart. For example, her natal Sun had progressed from Capricorn into Aries, suggesting that she had evolved into a more confident person and, because the progressed Sun was positioned at the eighth house, it suggests that she had become more emotionally intense than previously in her life. Aptly, the eighth house is associated with death and transformation and this could indicate that she had no fear of death, given that Aries' qualities include courageousness and optimism. Scorpio and its ruler, Pluto, are both connected with the eighth house in the natural zodiac and in Gill's progressed chart the Virgo ascendant had progressed into Scorpio. Given that the ascendant is associated with our physical appearance and projected personality, the progressed ascendant suggests that Gill may have become more controlling and obsessive, as well as having developed an increased perception. This is because these characteristics are associated with Scorpio and its ruler, Pluto. In her transits chart on the day that Gill died, transiting Pluto was conjunct the natal ascendant. This indicates that the Plutonian and Scorpion energy was exceptionally strong at that point in time and she must have been brutally aware that she was facing the inevitability of death.

To some people, Gill may have appeared even more mysterious and secretive than before. She was out of sight to the general public and her neighbours when she was in hospital for the last few months of her remaining life. However, the MC (Midheaven) had progressed into the creative and individual sign of Leo. This is shown when Gill, via her artwork, came into the spotlight significantly after her death, her talents were centre-stage and she became even more famous for her work, especially in artistic circles, and this will be discussed further on.

When she died, there were significant transits being made to her natal planets in the fifth house. The transits comprised of: transiting Sun conjunct Mercury; transiting Jupiter conjunct natal Venus; and transiting Saturn conjunct natal Sun and Venus. In medical astrology, the lungs are associated with Mercury – and this is pertinent to the transiting Sun conjunct natal Mercury showing that there was focus on Gill's breathing, chest and lungs. She died of bronchopneumonia, which is a type of pneumonia where the patient has problems with breathing due to inflammation of the alveoli.

Certainly, Gill will have been focused on matters of the mind and communication, especially if she could not express herself capably at this time. Possibly she would have been worried about Mercury associated subjects, such as important life decisions,

Author's photograph of the base of Madge Gill's grave (interred with her son, Leonard E. Gill) which reads: 'Peace Perfect Peace'.

correspondence and letters and plans for the future. She was probably concerned about the health of her sole surviving son (connected with the fifth house of children), Lawrence, who was ill and also in hospital himself around the same time that his mother was also in hospital.

Transiting Jupiter was at the fifth house and conjunct the natal Venus. This symbolises that Gill may have had spent her last few years pouring much energy and time into her creative activities and hobbies and that, through her relationship with art, she found the most pleasure in her life. Transiting Saturn was conjunct Gill's natal Sun and it restricts the energy of the Sun – which is fundamental life energy. The energy of Saturn confines and restricts, which suggests that Gill was very limited in what she could do in her last few years of life. Consequently, she may have felt even more isolated, lonely and cut off from people than previously.

Transiting Saturn conjunct natal Venus suggests that her relationships may have gone through a testing time, possibly this was true of her son, Lawrence. However, as it was a solid relationship between them, it was likely to have been able to have withstood any challenges and obstacles. It may have been another time of austerity for Gill and where she had to be cautious with finances. This may have led her to feel depressed and isolated. However, being the sensible Capricorn that she was, deprivation and vigilance were no stranger to her as, at an early age, she had experienced poverty and scarcity.

The transiting Sun at the fifth house was square the natal Saturn when Gill died. It emphasises the theme that she may have been feeling exhausted, frustrated and pessimistic, as these are all associations of Saturn. There may have been disappointments and sorrow with her family too. Gill went to hospital shortly before Christmas in 1960 and remained there until her death in January, 1961. Lawrence had his own health problems and was admitted to a different hospital in early January of 1961; there he remained until August of that same year (Dutton, 2019, 171). It must have been exceptionally distressing and sad for both Gill and Lawrence to be apart from each other when Gill was dying. Sadly, Lawrence died two years after his mother.

It has been observed that Gill "did not work in 'outsider' isolation, yet she remained for all her life an isolated spirit" (*Raw Vision*, 2015, 31/Ayad). In this description, we can see Gill's Capricorn energy at work through the loneliness and seclusion. Mercury is the ruling planet of her rectified natal chart, and we have addressed many of the associations connected with Mercury. An area that is missing, however, is that of humour, jesting and wit. Not only did Gill spend a lot of her time in isolation, particularly in her adult years, but there also seems to have been a lack of fun, joy and spontaneity in her life. If there was, there doesn't appear to be any anecdotes or evidence of it recorded anywhere by the few who did know her.

Black and white Mural of Madge Gill Painted by Pang of pang_artworks, found at the junction of Palmerston Road and Walthamstow High Street, E17.

Gill may have been unable to find humour in life, becoming excessively absorbed and serious in what she felt were her duties and obligations for her spirit-guide, involving her art and spiritual work. She could be forgiven for not being able to laugh, given what she had experienced in her lifetime. Harry Edwards concluded in his 'do's and dont's' counsel for mediums: "Be natural, enjoy humour and look for happiness in all things" (Edwards, 2003, 38). If Gill had been able to do this, her life may have been less devout which, in turn, may have created other opportunities for her, such as increasing her social life and not taking herself too seriously.

She inherited the ways of her mother, Emma Eades, in that, by and large, she lived her life in seclusion. During Gill's isolation, she produced an enormous amount of artwork and writing – over

Madge Gill née Maud Eades (Waltham Forest Heritage) by Spudgun67 – Licensed under CC by 2.0.

1000 pieces. When Lawrence Gill donated his mother's work to East Ham Council, the librarian, James Green, said that there were pieces of art that went back as far as 1919. He said that the pictures ranged in date from 1919 to 1958. He added that: "Some of the earlier ones almost precede the abstract school of art as we know it" (Dutton, 2019, 174). Madge Gill's rich inner life and her spirit guide, Myrninerest, of many years, coupled with her diligent attitude generated a driving force that enabled her to produce the best work that she possibly could. Such was her dutiful nature that the work she produced became an obligation (a quality associated with Capricorn) rather than a hobby or pastime. Her compulsion may also have been for spiritual companionship with Myrninerest and ultimately for her God.

Both Gill and her son, Lawrence, were correct in their belief that, one day in the far future, after Gill had died, her art and creations would receive accolade and be celebrated. This came to fruition, as she was featured in both group and solo shows. Examples include the following: in 1968 the Grosvenor Gallery in Mayfair, London held *The Guided Hand* exhibition, solely on Madge Gill's art. Then, in 1978, Roger Cardinal and Michael Thevos curated *Madge Gill at the Collection de l'Art Brut* in Switzerland. In 1979, the Hayward Gallery in Waterloo, London, presented *Outsiders – An Art without Precedent or Tradition*. It was curated by Roger Cardinal and Victor Musgrave and was arranged by the Arts Council of Great Britain (www.madegill.com).

In 2013, the Orleans House Gallery in Twickenham, London, exhibited *Madge Gill: Medium & Visionary*. The event was supported by the Wellcome Trust; a charitable organisation whose discovery research includes mental health. The focal point of the exhibition was a rarely-seen piece called *Crucifixion of the Soul*. It is an impressive ten metres long calico covered in Gill's trademark beautiful creativity, coupled with darkness and detail. The exhibition was curated by Mark De Novellis in collaboration with Henry Boxer, Roger Cardinal and Vivienne Roberts (www.madegill.com).

In 2019, the William Morris Gallery in Walthamstow, London, exhibited *Madge Gill by Myrninerest* and it was curated by Sophie Dutton. Accompanying the exhibition was a book published by Rough Trade Books called, *Madge Gill by Myrninerest*.

In 2021, Gill was featured in an exhibition at the Barbican Art Gallery in London, which celebrated the work of French artist, Jean Dubuffet, who died in 1985. The event was called *Jean Dubuffet: Brutal Beauty*. The exhibition advocated his rebellious philosophy and also his experimental work, "he tried to capture the poetry of everyday life in a gritty and more authentic way" (ibid). His principle forever remained the same: "Art should always make you laugh a little and fear a little anything but bore" (ibid). The event exhibited not only Dubuffet's work but also art from his collection of 'Art Brut' – this was a term that he created and it means 'raw art'.

There have been many more exhibitions both in England and abroad featuring Madge Gill and detail about them can be found on the excellent website: www.madgegill.com which was founded by Vivienne Roberts, the current archivist and curator at the College of Psychic Studies. Madge Gill has also been featured in several exhibitions held at the College of Psychic Studies in South Kensington, London, and has been the subject of an online talk in 2021, given by Vivienne Roberts called *The Art of Madge Gill: Myrinerest, Marconi and Mars*. Earlier, in 1985, the prestigious auctioneers, Christies (also in South Kensington), held an auction devoted to the works of Madge Gill. It was called *Watercolours and Drawings by Madge Gill* (www.madgegill.com).

Vivienne Roberts observed that demand for Gill's work has led to a recent increase in prices. For example, at an auction in 2017, it was recorded that a nine foot calico drawing achieved over £37,000 and a *Daily Telegraph* report claimed that some have even changed hands for close to £100,000 (*LIGHT*, 2019, Vol.140, 20). Although there is tremendous commercial success in Madge Gill becoming a highly collectable artist, one other area remains constant ... Madge Gill, Myrinerest and her art and automatic writing remain as mysterious as they ever were and just perhaps that is the way she wanted it and still wants it.

ACKNOWLEDGMENTS, CREDITS & REFERENCES

THANKS TO:
- Ayshea Ahmed, author and illustrator of *The Wonderful World of Madge Gill – Outsider Artist and Visionary*, for her passion for astrology and enthusiasm for this piece of writing, as well as her kindness in granting me permission to use the postcard of Madge Gill's artwork, *Lady in a Hat*, which she owns.
- The genius book, *Madge Gill by Myrninerest*, edited by Sophie Dutton, which provides access not only to Madge Gill's artwork but also insightful perspectives from those that knew her or knew of her.

Mick Frankel, devisor of *The Deck of the Hebrew Letters* (artwork by James Douglas), for information regarding caretaking at synagogues, as well as information about Hebrew letters and their correspondences found in some of Madge Gill's automatic writing.

Special thanks to M.B. Jackson (author of *Sigils*), for his knowledge, observations and helpful discussions about Madge Gill's automatic writing, ancient scripts and sigils.

Much appreciation to Vivienne Roberts for her meticulous website: www.madgegill.com and for the superb special edition of *LIGHT* magazine dedicated to *The Art and Spirit of Madge Gill*, as well as her generosity of spirit, knowledge and passion for Madge Gill.

BHCARA (British Home Children in Canada) – huge thanks to Lori Oschefski, for information on survivors sailing as steerage passengers and their illnesses. Also for her kindness in granting me permission to publish her photograph of where Madge Gill worked for Mr and Mrs Rae.

Ian Black, for sharing the Ancestry.co.uk / National Records Office knowledge with me on dates on various subjects regarding the Eades family.

City of London Cemetery administration staff for assisting me to find the burial plot for Madge Gill.

Barts National Health Trust – the archivist, for information about duties undertaken at the Union Workhouses.

The Museum Curator at the College of Optometrists, for information about the practical details of living with glass eyes in the 1920s, and for the photograph of the box of glass eyes.

Redbridge Museum and Heritage Centre archivist, for information about the 1918 rate book for Fern Cottage, George Lane in Wanstead, as well as granting license for the photo of Barnardo's Girl's Village, showing the church.

Senior Research Officer at SANDS (the Stillbirth and Neonatal Deaths) national charity, for information about stillbirths in the 1900s and how parents were treated during that period.

The Archives Manager at Making Connections Barnardo's, for information regarding employment and pay levels to children in Canada on the British Home Schemes. Also for granting license to use the photograph of Maud Eades as a Barnardo's child.

The Heritage Manager at the Newham Local History & Archives, for facilitating my visit to the archives and organising license for me to use the Madge Gill postcard from their collection of Madge Gill's postcards.

ASTROLOGY SECOND SIGHT ART

The Heritage Officer at the Newham Local History & Archives, for dates and information about the origins of three spiritualist churches in the borough.

The Keep, East Sussex Record Office archivists, for assistance with Gill's Medical Records.

Birth Certificate for Madge Gill:
General Records Office: Volume 4a, page 223, West Ham District. 19th January, 1882.

Death Certificate for Madge Gill:
General Records Office: Volume 5a, page 204, in the sub-district of Leyton in the County of Essex. Informant: Samuel Faust (unknown if it was a friend or hospital employee). Cause of death: Bronchopneumonia. Died on 28th January, 1961, at Langthorne Hospital, Leytonstone.

Burial Site for Madge Gill:
Plot number 116615 – square 62, for Madge Gill, interred with her son, Leonard E. Gill (who died in 1950), near Anchor Road and Ford's Circle, at the City of London Cemetery and Crematorium, Aldersbrook Road, Manor Park, E12 5DQ.

Birth Certificate for Tom Edwin Gill:
General Records Office: Volume 1b, page 605, St. Giles South District.

Death Certificate for Tom Edwin Gill:
General Records Office: Volume 4a, page 366, West Ham District.

Service Record for Thomas Gill:
National Archives: Service Records: ADM-188/617/28889.

Birth Certificate for Emma Eades:
General Records Office: Volume 2a, page 56, Guildford District.

Death Certificate for Emma Eades:
General Records Office: Volume 4a, page 409, West Ham District.

ASTROLOGY DETAIL

Natal chart generated by: www.astro.com (Astro-dienst).
Rodden Rating Classification is 'X' for the natal chart based on rectification method.
Eades, M. Born on Thursday 19th January, 1882, at 20.00pm (rectified), Walthamstow, England, UK.
Co-ordinates 0w02, 51n34.

BOOKS

Ahmed. A. (2020) *The Wonderful World of Madge Gill – Outsider Artist and Visionary.* Cranthorpe Millner Publishers.
Bayley, H. (1912) *The Lost Language of Symbolism Volume 1.* Bracken Books London.
Cardinal, R. (1972) *Outsider Art.* Praeger Publishers, Inc.
Carrington, H. (1975) *Your Psychic Powers and How To Develop Them.* Newcastle Publishing Co., Inc.
Dutton, S. (2019) *Madge Gill by Myrinerest.* Rough Trade Books.
Edwards. H. (2003) *A Guide for the Development of Mediumship.* Con-Psy Publications Middlesex.
Hodgson, J. (2005) *Wisdom in the Stars.* White Eagle Publishing Trust.
Jackson, M.B. (2021) *Sigils: Illustrated Guide to the Symbols of Spirit and Thought.* Green Magic Publishing.
Miles, A.J. (2022) *Famous Occultists and Witches – Their Biographies and Birth Charts.* Green Magic Publishing.
Parker, J & D. (1991) *Parker's Astrology: The Definitive Guide to Using Astrology in Every Aspect of Your Life.* Dorling Kindersley Limited.
Reinhart, M. (1989) *Chiron and the Healing Journey: An Astrological and Psychological Perspective.* Arkarna Contemporary Astrology.
Rhodes, C. (2000) *Outsider Art – Spontaneous Alternatives.* Thames & Hudson.

JOURNALS

The Lancet (http://www.thelancet.com), Volume 395, 11th April, 2020, by Georgina Ferry.
'A Woman's Place – Helen Boyle: Pioneer of Early Mental Health Treatment.'

MAGAZINES

LIGHT (June 2019), Volume 140. Published by the College of Psychic Studies.
The Art and Spirit of Madge Gill – Special Edition of *LIGHT*.
Raw Vision (2015), Issue No.87, pages 26–33 / **Ayad, S.** *Mine Worker's Hands: The Arts and Crafting of Madge Gill (1882–1961)*. Photographs by Edward Russell Westwood.

NEWSPAPERS

Psychic News, 18th July, 1942, page 3, "'Unseen' Forces Guide Artist."

PDFS

Camic, P.M. (2013) *Madge Gill Catalogue* – Essay Chapter: *Toward Wellbeing Creativity and Resilience in the Life and Work of Madge Gill.* Madge Gill retrospective exhibition catalogue. Orleans House Gallery, London, 2013.

REPORTS

Medical Report for Madge Gill from the Lady Chichester Hospital for Women and Children, including notes from previous doctors in 1921, as well as Dr Helen Boyle at the Lady Chichester Hospital in 1922 (from January 1922 – April 1922).

WEBSITES

https://www.academia.edu/3030103/_Cosmic_Cavalcade_Madge_Gill_and_the_East_End_Academies_1932_1947 – Gary Haines: information about Madge's sons exhibiting at the Whitechapel Gallery, as well as the quote from Madge when she went to the gallery before the exhibition started. Accessed on 15/11/2022.
https://archives.innertemple.org.uk/names/browse/admissions/surname/N -Search for 'Nunn'. Accessed on 12/08/2022.

https://www.bartshealth.nhs.uk – Details of nurses at the West Ham Union Infirmary, information about the Hackney Union Infirmary and details about Langthorne Hospital in the 1960s. Accessed on 12/08/2022.

https://www.bethsnotesplus.com/2017/02/home-sweet-home.html – For lyrics of the song, *Home Sweet Home*. Accessed on 11/10/2022.

https://www.british-history.ac.uk/vch/essex/vol6/pp123-141#h3-0017 – Information about when spiritualist churches near to Madge Gill's home were founded. Accessed on 03/08/2022.

https://www.britishhomechildren.com/heritage-links-for-research – ALLAN LINE OF ROYAL MAIL STEAMERS: passenger lists for Maud Eades' journey to and from Canada. Accessed on 03/09/2022.

https://canadianbritishhomechildren.weebly.com/childrens-trunks--bibles.html – Information about Bibles and prayer books. Accessed on 18/09/2022.

https://www.freebmd.org.uk/cgi/districts.pl?r=131207211:9057&d=bmd_1653949805 – Information on the date of the death of Walter Eades. Accessed on 25/09/2022.

http://health.hackneysociety.org/page_id__246.aspx?path=0p2p39p – The Story of Healthcare in Hackney, Nursing Regulations 1897, *Hackney Union Infirmary* by Sue Kinder. Accessed on 17/09/2022.

https://heritage.canadiana.ca/view/oocihm.lac_reel_c4715/1418 – Information regarding The Home Children Scheme and its' heritage. Accessed on 03/09/2022.

https://historicengland.org.uk/research/inclusive-heritage/disability-history/1914-1945/everyday-life-and-work – Information about 'feeble-mindedness'. Accessed on 17/10/2022.

https://historicengland.org.uk/research/current/discover-and-understand/military/the-first-world-war/first-world-war-home-front/what-we-already-know/air/first-blitz – Information on the First Blitz hitting infant school in Poplar, East London. Accessed on 26/11/2022.

https://www.history.com/news/steerage-act-immigration-19th-century – Information about steerage conditions on the ships. Accessed on 03/09/2022.

http://www.madgegill.com – For meticulous information on the biography and chronology of Madge Gill's life. Accessed on 03/09/2022.

https://www.mind.org.uk/about-us/our-achievements – Information about the charity Mind's timeline and the formation of it. Accessed on 31/08/2022.

https://museumofthemind.org.uk/blog/diligent-detective-work-2-the-copyright-mystery-of-madge-gill – Information showing Madge

Gill as the subject of a blog for the Bethlem Museum of the Mind. Accessed on 29/10/2022.

https://www.nationalarchives.gov.uk – Service record for Thomas Edwin Gill, Ref: ADM 188/617/28889. Accessed on 13/09/2022.

https://www.newhamheritagemonth.org/records/madge-gill-inspired-dye-workshop-with-artist-lola-lely – Madge Gill quote about being a man and studying botany. Accessed on 17/10/2022.

https://www.nhs.uk/Services/Hospitals/Overview/DefaultView.aspx?id=3093 – The oldest psychiatric hospital in the world. Accessed on 25/10/2022.

https://www.npg.org.uk/collections/search/person/mp96349/alice-helen-anne-boyle – Information about Dr Boyle's career. Accessed on 27/08/2022.

https://www.pewresearch.org -Information on diversity breakdown in India: 'Religion in India'. Accessed on 12/11/2022.

https://recherche-collection-search.bac-lac.gc.ca – Government of Canada. Information on Hazelbrae Home, Peterborough, Ontario. Accessed on 03/09/2022.

https://www.tate.org.uk/art/art-terms/o/outsider-art – Definition of 'Outsider Art'. Accessed on 27/10/2022.

https://en.wikipedia.org/wiki/Home!_Sweet_Home!#:~:text – Origins about the song, *Home Sweet Home*. Accessed on 17/09/2022.

Glossary of Terms

Adama: John Dee in his journals also referred to the 'language of angels' as Adamical. According to Dee's angels, it was used by Adam in Paradise to name all things.

Aspect: is an angle the planets make to each other in the horoscope, as well as with the Ascendant, Midheaven, Descendant and Lower Heaven (IC). Major aspects comprise of: conjunction, opposition, sextile, square and trine angles.

Axis: the angles in a chart where the Ascendant, Imum Coeli (IC), Descendant and Midheaven (MC) are positioned.

Chiron: is an asteroid and in astrology it symbolises the 'Wounded Healer' – it represents our deepest wounds and endeavours to heal them. Chiron orbits the Sun between Saturn and Uranus.

Clairaudient: means the ability to hear sounds said to exist beyond the reach of ordinary experience.

Clairvoyance: means 'clear-seeing' and is a type of psychic gift, which allows the psychic to see the hidden.

Critical degrees: the degrees of 0 and 29 in a sign; they are critical because they are the first and final degree.

Detriment: a planet which is positioned in the zodiac sign opposite the sign it rules.

Descendant: the Descendant is the cusp of the seventh house.

Draconic astrology: an ancient system which helps an individual to realise their spiritual purpose in life and the challenges they may encounter along the way.

Enochian language: the term comes from John Dee's assertion that the biblical patriarch, Enoch, was the last human (before Dee and Kelley) to know the language of the angels.

Ephemeris: is a book of planetary positions that lists where the planets will be in the zodiac in the past, present or future.

Exaltation: each of the seven traditional planets has its exaltation in one zodiac sign; the Sun in Aries, the Moon in Taurus, Mercury in Virgo, Venus in Pisces, Mars in Capricorn, Jupiter in Cancer and Saturn in Libra.

Flat chart: is a chart which only shows the aspects and planets with no house system, as the time of birth is unknown.

Focal point: the squared planet or point in a T-Square (see below for T-Square definition).

Grand Trine: a Grand Trine consists of three planets that occupy different signs of the same element at 120 degree angles.

Hard aspect: refers to major angles created between planets, which comprise of the conjunction, opposition and square angles (n.b. the conjunction is variable depending on the energies of the two planets involved).

Houses: a house in the natal chart reveals 'where' planetary energies express themselves. Each of the twelve houses in a chart rule certain areas of life, types of people and relationships, ideas and circumstances of life.

Imum Coeli/IC: Coeli is Latin for 'Bottom of the Sky'. The Imum Coeli is the 'nadir' or low point in the Sun's path and (if you could see the Sun) where it would be seen at midnight, it is also the cusp of the fourth house.

Inconjunction: is a minor aspect which creates an angle of 150 degrees with another planet.

Major aspects: comprise of conjunction, opposition, sextile, square and trine angles.

Midheaven/MC Coeli: is Latin for 'heaven'. Medium Coeli is the Midheaven and is the where the Sun would be at noon at the top of the chart, it is also the tenth house cusp.

Minor aspects: comprise of inconjunction, semi-sextile, semi-square and sesquiquadrate angles.

Modes: there are three modes in astrology which are represented by cardinal, fixed and mutable energies. They all represent the way in which a sign operates. Cardinal signs are initiators of action and are the signs Aries, Cancer, Libra and Capricorn. Fixed signs have staying power and are the signs Taurus, Leo, Scorpio and Aquarius. Mutable signs have a versatile attitude and are the signs Gemini, Virgo, Sagittarius and Pisces.

Moon's Nodes: North and South Nodes. The Moons Nodes theorise that one is born with overdeveloped and underdeveloped traits of our character. The North Node indicates traits which we need to develop in order to find inner happiness, and the South Node indicates the overdeveloped traits which we are comfortable with and retain for security purposes. The North Node is also known as the Dragon's Head and the South Node the Dragon's Tail.

Mutual reception: is when two planets are in each other's sign of rulership. For example, Saturn in Scorpio and Pluto in Capricorn.

GLOSSARY OF TERMS

Natal chart: a natal chart is a picture of the positions of the signs, planets and angles at the time of one's birth. It contains data such as date, time and place of birth to generate an accurate astrological chart.

Natural zodiac: is a system where the twelve signs of the zodiac are assimilated into the twelve houses in the birth chart, given that they have similar characteristics. For example, the first sign, Aries, is associated with the first house – they both being about the self. The second sign, Taurus, is associated with the second house, given that Taurus is about possessions and the second house is about resources; and so on.

Progressions: a system where astrologers equate one day after birth to one year of life, known as 'the year for the day method.'

Rectification: This involves looking at significant events in a person's life and calculating the transiting outer planets in the natal chart and interpreting any aspects (particularly with the natal personal planets). From the process of rectification, a birth time can be concluded.

Rodden Rating System: a system developed by astrologer, Lois Rodden, which classifies astrological data by grade to reflect its accuracy for research and purposes for astrologers. Classification starts at 'AA' then 'A' and finishes at 'XX' – for further details see: https://www.astro.com/astro-databank/help:RR

Stellium: multiple conjunctions of planets, a close cluster of three or more planets in one sign and/or house.

Transits: the planets continue their movement and complete their cycles, they form special relationships to the planets and points in our individual natal charts.

T-Square: is a pattern formed when planets in opposition also form a square with another planet. The pattern resembles the letter 'T' when viewed in the chart. The squared planet or point is referred to as the release point. T-Squares are made of up of each of the modes: cardinal, fixed and mutable.

www.ingramcontent.com/pod-product-compliance
Lightning Source LLC
Chambersburg PA
CBHW070804100426
42742CB00012B/2240